When Storms Come

Discovering Hope in Adversity

Chuck Smith

world
PUBLISHING
SINCE 1928

Contents

Foreword

Chuck Smith, Jr.

One blustery night in 1958, I stood huddled with my family near a small fence, eagerly waiting and watching the sky. There weren't many people around as we gathered at the Orange County (CA) Airport (now known as John Wayne Airport), which was then little more than a flight school and parking lot for private planes. Every Sunday cars raced down one of the runways, which served as the first commercial drag strip until 1959, when it was closed due to increased air traffic.

That night, however, we were there to greet Grandpa and Uncle Bill the minute they climbed out of the single-engine plane they were flying from Victorville. In those days, there were no metal detectors or security officers, and we could have easily strolled onto the tarmac.

Grandma was there when we arrived. Jan, my older sister; Jeff, my younger brother; and I greeted her with a hug. She smiled warmly at Mom and Dad, grateful for the adult company while she waited for her two heroes to complete their maiden flight and arrive home safely. Grandpa was the consummate gentleman from a more polite and romantic era; Uncle Bill was the baby of the family who had grown up to be a type-T motorcycle racer and daredevil. I do not remember being aware of Grandma's anxiety, but looking back now I realize all three adults must have been holding their breath, nervous about the flight.

When the hour had long passed for the plane and its pilots to come motoring through the sky, Dad surmised they had been delayed. He told Grandma, "Mom, you need to get home and stay by the phone so they can reach you. We'll take the kids home and get them ready for bed, but give us a call as soon as you hear from them and we will rush back to welcome them with you." We had been home only a few minutes when the phone rang. Grandma said Bill had called to explain how they veered off course and landed in San Diego. The remainder of the flight would be easy because they would simply follow the lights along the Pacific Coast Highway until they reached Newport Beach. "We'll be landing in about an hour," he promised. What a relief!

We bundled up and returned to the airport. Again we waited. I remember a small plane landing, and my brother, sister, and I started shouting at the two men who emerged from the door. But they were not Grandpa and Uncle Bill.

The hour Bill promised came and went. We kept peering into the empty sky and straining our eyes and ears for a sign of the plane that would bring our intrepid aviators home to us. Again we had to leave the airport disappointed; only this time Dad was more apprehensive than earlier. The airport was mostly dark, as were the surrounding fields and neighborhoods. Today I wonder why that night had to be so surreal. The wind howled and the long branches of the trees around our house bent over and shuddered as if aware of some great sadness.

I was awakened by the phone ringing around 5:30 the next morning. When I stepped out of my room into the hallway, there was very little sound or light, and I thought no one else was up or awake. But I looked toward the front of the house, and silhouetted against the large picture window was our dining room table, the phone sitting on it with the receiver in its cradle. Dad had his back to me and his hands were cupped over his face. I stood and watched for a moment, but he sat as still as death.

Within a day or two, Dad had to identify the bodies of his father and kid brother. Before then, I do not remember ever seeing tears in his eyes, nor did I see him cry again until many years later. I do not remember him ever breaking down; in fact, he stepped on the platform that next Sunday and delivered his sermon just as he had every Sunday for as long as I had been alive. But tears were in his eyes when looping his necktie, and again when he walked from the front door of our house to the front door of the church adjacent to our yard. His voice caught so that he had to pause once or twice before he could complete his sermon.

Some of us think others live a charmed life while *we* get all the pain and garbage. But a wise man once said, *"The heart knows its own bitterness"* (Prov. 14:10).

We have no way of knowing what the optimistic, happy—or *blessed*—person has survived, what he must overcome every day, what he carries with him. We do know, however, some people survive unbelievable loss and pain, yet thrive and exude joy, while others suffer a minor setback and never recover.

I tell you the story of my grandfather's and uncle's passing (and my grandmother's later death by cancer was equally sad) so you would appreciate Dad's personal experience in the *valley of the shadow of death (Ps. 23:4)*. While reading through this book you might be tempted to think what he proposes is too simple; he should go deeper into the nature of suffering; or he should offer suggestions for a holistic approach to hardship, heartache, and despair. Being a person who tends to probe deeply into issues, I sometimes find the best answers and remedies were lying on the surface, all the while I was trudging in the mire.

Dad has suffered and struggled, known loss and wept at grave sites, been stricken with pain and even today, like Jacob after his encounter with God at the Jabok River, walks with a limp. Yet each morning, he rises to a God-filled world and steps into it with unshakable faith, unbeatable hope, and unquenchable joy. I still need to learn much from him, and I am thankful he has shared with us a few of his secrets in this encouraging book. He is one of those people who can teach us how to rise above our circumstances, live with what life gives us, and, when we suffer, continue to press forward, singing the praise of God. Does life wound, scar, devastate, and oppress? Yes, Yes, and Yes. But please read this book with an open heart, for the one who speaks has learned from Scripture how one can be *sorrowful yet always rejoicing (2 Cor. 6:10, NASB)*.

Prayer

Thank You, Father, for being everything
we could ever need and more.
In Your love we find
courage to face every threat,
strength to meet every challenge,
and hope to rise to every opportunity.
We rest in You,
confident that all things are under Your control,
and knowing You work all things together for
our good.
Now we open our hearts to Your Word,
asking You to instruct us in faith,
nurture us in love,
assure us through Your Spirit,
to know fully Your rule over the world
so we can live free from worry and fear.
Thank You for the work of Your truth in
our souls.
In Jesus' name.
Amen.

CHAPTER 1

Conquering Fear

"Go, gather all the Jews who are present in Shushan, and fast for me; neither eat nor drink for three days, night or day. My maids and I will fast likewise. And so will I go in unto the king, which is against the law; and if I perish, I perish!"

(Esth. 4:16)

LIVING IN PROVIDENCE

When was the last time you heard someone use the word *providence*? People used to talk about God's providence all the time, but you hardly hear it mentioned anymore. The preferred word today is *serendipity*. Perhaps providence suggests God's control over the natural world, whereas serendipity is merely a fortunate accident. There is a world of difference between *providence* and *serendipity*.

Serendipity is nothing more than luck. You cannot rely on serendipity; you can only feel relief or pleasure when circumstances work to your advantage. Providence, however, has nothing to do with luck, but everything to do with a God who in His wisdom, power, and love, works through the objects and forces of the natural world to achieve His purpose. You can trust God that in His providence He will arrange your circumstances to accomplish His will—using even unwanted events that otherwise seem like disaster.

Serendipity is uncertain, providence is absolute; serendipity is unpredictable, providence is guaranteed; serendipity is impersonal, providence is the design of a Heavenly Father who has your best interests at heart. If you are hoping for serendipity, you have every reason to be anxious, fearful, and unsure about the future. If you trust in God to exercise His providence over your life and circumstances, you can rest your soul in hope, faith, and peace.

The Book of Esther is a story of God's providence at work in the life of a young woman whom He used to rescue her people and change the world. Before she was ever selected to audition before Ahasuerus, king of Persia; before she was chosen to become the queen; before she learned that the lives of her people were in jeopardy, God made her *lovely and beautiful (Esth. 2:7)*. Esther grew up as an attractive young woman. Was there a time in her childhood or teenage years when she could have ever imagined a practical purpose for her beauty? Did she have a flicker of insight regarding the combination of her beauty and destiny? Probably not. She was most likely unaware she was lovely by God's design as well as destined to turn around an entire nation.

We cannot see God's providence today; we can only see our circumstances. We cannot imagine how God will use our weaknesses and strengths, our successes and failures, our talents and defects to produce the outcome He desires. We can, however, trust His sovereign rule over all things, whether good or bad. Nothing can prevent God from achieving His objectives in the world.

Esther's cousin, Mordecai, had the wisdom to discern the possibility that her extraordinary rise to the throne was *for such a time as this (Esth. 4:14)*. In other words, he began to put together the pieces of the puzzle so God's providence rose to the surface of their circumstances and became visible. Esther was fortunate to have someone in her life to provide this service for her—to help her see how each phase of her early life and present situation fit into a divine plan.

If we rewind Esther's story back to an earlier episode, we can see why God's providence and timing were so critical in her life. In the first chapter of Esther, we see the king in a fit over Vashti's (his current wife) refusal to show off her beauty in front of his dinner guests. After the king banished her, his advisers recommended that he stock his harem with hundreds of the world's most beautiful women and choose one of them to replace Vashti as queen. Of all those women, Esther was the one who won the king's heart.

"As providence would have it," so to speak, Esther's cousin overheard an assassination plot, and he told Esther, who informed the king in Mordecai's name. An investigation was launched, and Mordecai's patriotic deed was recorded. But not everyone was pleased with Mordecai. The king's courtier, Haman, resented Mordecai for not bowing down to him when he passed through the gates of the palace. When Haman began plotting his revenge, he discovered Mordecai was Jewish, so Haman decided to eradicate all Jews. Little did he know that Queen Esther was also Jewish (an identity she hid on Mordecai's advice) and that she was his nemesis' cousin.

When Mordecai heard of Haman's program against the Jews—which the king signed into indisputable law—he began to mourn outside the palace gate. When Esther heard of Mordecai's grief, they began to send messages back and forth. He counseled her to use her royal status to plead with the king for the lives of her people, but she responded that approaching the king uninvited could result in instant execution. Mordecai reminded her that she was as good as dead anyway, and the very fact she was queen could be for this specific purpose and time. That is when she decided to go to the king and make the courageous statement, " . . . *if I perish, I perish" (Esth. 4:16).*

At that moment, neither Esther nor Mordecai knew for certain this was her moment of destiny and the outworking of God's providence. Therefore, she set aside all concern for her own safety and committed to risk her life for her people. She had to act fearlessly in the face of a very real and deadly threat.

CHRISTIAN CONFIDENCE

Jesus called His followers to a life free from fear. He gave assurance the purposes of God were bigger than all of life's worries. In fact, worry can interfere with the effectiveness of God's Word in our lives (see Mark

4:19). In the Sermon on the Mount, where the bulk of Jesus' teaching on worry and fear appears, He says, *"Therefore do not worry about tomorrow, for tomorrow will worry about its own things. Sufficient for the day is its own trouble" (Matt. 6:34).*

Nevertheless, many Christians *do* worry about tomorrow. Though Paul tells believers not to be anxious about *anything* (see Phil. 4:6), Christians are anxious about *many* things. Scripture says repeatedly, *"Do not fear,"* yet people who claim to believe the Bible and live by its teaching find themselves haunted by any number of fears.

Jesus wants His people to understand God's heart—that He cares for us so we can live without anxious care. God does not want us to be hounded by worries, eaten up with anxieties, or constrained by fears. He wants us to be free from all these forms of emotional imprisonment so we might *serve Him without fear, in holiness and righteousness before Him all the days of our life (Luke 1:74).*

SURRENDER TO YOUR DESTINY

Esther's life focused on one specific moment of destiny. A divine plan that spanned the ages and world continents made her life and personal concerns seem insignificant. That plan hinged on the cruel ambition of one insane man, and the opportunity to undo his evil fell to Esther. The pivotal point of God's work in her time rested on her decision to risk everything. Her life, the history of God's people, and the revelation of His salvation would soon be understood in light of this decisive moment. Behind the scenes, God's providence was at work in the royal courts of Persia, moving Esther into a critical position of political leverage. But she had to choose to take her life in her own hands. Once God's will was fulfilled, everything in Esther's life would make sense.

Do you suppose Esther saw her destiny with perfect clarity? Of course not. At least not when she made that terrible decision. If she had been certain of her destiny, she would not have said, " . . . *if I perish, I perish.*" She did not know the king would accept her, the tables would be turned on Haman, or that Mordecai would be elevated to a position of power and honor. Esther had to determine that fears regarding her personal safety could not keep her from doing whatever she could to save her people, even at the risk of her own life.

We do not always recognize our moment of decision, the hour of destiny, or the position we occupy in God's eternal plan. Rather than surrender ourselves to what we must do to promote God's will, we struggle to control the outcome of our circumstances and decisions. We want a guarantee that if we make the right choice, we *will* survive, and that honor and blessings will follow. But since we are *not* the center of the universe, we forfeit God's peace whenever we insist that everything go our way. Fighting for control will always throw us into in a state of conflict and turmoil.

Do you ever find yourself amazed at your ability to invent worries? We can torture ourselves with the "What-ifs?": *What if we run out of money? What if there is a food shortage? What if we cannot buy gasoline? What if I lose my job, my health, or my retirement? What if, what if, what if?* Esther's "What if?" was very real and dangerous: "What if the king does not extend the scepter and acknowledge me?" Not only would her plan fail but she would lose her life. However, she was able to respond to this question with a courageous declaration: " . . . *if I perish, I perish.*"

How can we find this same resolve to simply *do* God's will? The answer is *surrender*. We need to be clear on this term, because it does not mean we *resign* ourselves to an intolerable situation or that we take the fatalistic attitude of Thomas, who went even further with "What if?," to certain doom, *"Let us also go, that we may die with Him" (John 11:16).* Surrender does not mean we fall into a void hoping for a soft landing. Surrender is an expression of our trust in God, a trust in His love, goodness, power, and wisdom.

When you make the decision to surrender to God's will, you are liberated from worry and anxiety. To trust God enough to surrender to His plan and His future means that our lives are anchored to a hope beyond this life. If we must take a huge risk, we know at least that the worst that can happen to us is that we die. But when we die—and we all will, though some will die in the thick of God's will and others will die resisting it—we will be with the God to whom we have surrendered, which is not too bad at all. The kind of surrender that overcomes worry is the fearless trust in God that says not to *fear those who kill the body but cannot kill the soul (Matt. 10:28).*

Try saying these words aloud: "Lord, my life is in

Your hands. I commit all the important issues of life and death to You. I will not worry about the risks of doing Your will any longer. Instead, I will trust You to take care of me, because you are my Father and I am Your child."

An Old Woman and a Big God

I was still a young man when Kay and I moved to Huntington Beach, California, to take over a small church. One of my official duties was visitation, those times when I would make my rounds through the community dropping in on people in their homes—mostly the elderly who were unable to attend our services. However, I have to admit I went to see one person more frequently than others because she did far more to build my faith than I could ever do for her.

She was in her 90s and had walked with the Lord most of her life. Her relationship with Jesus Christ was so deep and rich that every word she spoke was tinged with divine intimacy. I am convinced that God graced her with a gift of encouragement. Several times I went to her home feeling a little discouraged. Then she would remind me: "God has not vacated His throne, and He is still in control!" I would take heart knowing her life had not been easy and she spoke with the wisdom of experience.

In those early days of ministry I had a tendency to forget God was on the throne. Whenever we ran into problems—feeling the full responsibility of being the pastor—I would wonder, "What are we going to do?" Then I would find my way to her front door, and in her gentle and slightly raspy voice she would say, "Well, Charles, God is still on the throne, and He is still in control. God will take care of this problem, and you don't have to worry for Him." My heart would rejoice every time I grabbed hold of her words. In fact, I realized that even if the problems were not resolved to everyone's liking and the ministry failed, God was *still* on the throne and would see to the circumstances He allowed to develop. I am grateful she was there to teach me these lessons early in my ministry.

Looking back on the early years, I can say I had many more worries in that church of 100 people than I have now. In fact, I have not experienced worry in many years. God is on the throne, He's in control, and He will take care of me and guarantee His will in my life. Even if I wanted to, I could not change too many situations. I have learned to *cast all of my anxiety on him, because he cares for me (1 Pet. 5:7, NIV)*. His job is to command; mine—and yours—is to obey.

"I Love Ya Tomorrow"

I remember from my childhood a gospel song by Ira Stanphill, "I Know Who Holds Tomorrow." The chorus says:

> Many things about tomorrow
> I don't seem to understand,
> But I know Who holds tomorrow
> And I know Who holds my hand.

Do you find it interesting that most of our worries are located in tomorrow? Why worry about today if I am here and have enough money for lunch? God has brought me this far. But what about next week? What might happen then? Today is not so much of a challenge because we are here. But worry tends to be futuristic. Perhaps that is why Jesus did not want us to worry about tomorrow, because we have a tendency to project our fears into the future, then spoil today with worry.

Read carefully the words of Jesus:

> Therefore I say to you, do not worry about
> your life, what you will eat; nor about the
> body, what you will put on. Life is more
> than food, and the body is more than
> clothing. Consider the ravens, for they
> neither sow nor reap, which have neither
> storehouse nor barn; and God feeds them.
> Of how much more value are you than the
> birds? And which of you by worrying can
> add one cubit to his stature? If you then are
> not able to do the least, why are you
> anxious for the rest? Consider the lilies,
> how they grow: they neither toil, nor spin;
> and yet I say to you, even Solomon in all of
> his glory was not arrayed like one of these.
> If then God so clothes the grass, which
> today is in the field and tomorrow is
> thrown into the oven, how much more will
> He clothe you, O you of little faith?
> And do not seek what you shall eat or
> what you should drink, nor have an

anxious mind. For all these things the
nations of the world seek after, and your
Father knows that you need these things.
But seek the kingdom of God, and all these
things shall be added to you.

Do not fear, little flock, for it is your
Father's good pleasure to give you the
kingdom (Luke 12:22-32, see also Matt.
6:25-34).

Instead of worry, Jesus instructs us first to know our
Father knows all about us, including all our needs.
Second, our Heavenly Father is a gracious Provider
who even feeds the birds. You are not a bird, but the
Father's child, so how much more will He feed you?
He provides a beautiful wardrobe for grass in the
fields, which in a day or two is worthless. How much
more will He cover your eternal soul?

Here is a bit of biblical wisdom: *There is no fear in
love; but perfect love casts out fear (1 John 4:18).* Fear is a
symptom of a malfunction; when I fear, it is because I
do not realize how much God loves me. If I knew
God's love completely, perfectly, then I would not be
afraid. As long as God is on the throne, we have no
reason to fear. Now if God were to vacate the throne,
we would all be in big trouble. You might as well forget it; the game is over.

IF I PERISH . . .

During World War II, Japanese forces had taken the
Philippines and pressed the United States Navy in

the battle of Midway and other Pacific islands. Nazi armies had marched through Europe, and there seemed to be no way to halt the destructive jugger-naut. Life all over the world was bleak, but many North American churches persevered with a chorus written by Wendell P. Loveless in 1940: "I Have Christ In My Heart."

> What though wars may come with
>   marching feet and beat of the drum,
> For I have Christ in my heart.
> What though nations rage as we approach
>   the end of the age,
> For I have Christ in my heart.
> God is still on the throne, Almighty God Is
>   He;
> And He cares for His own through all
>   eternity,
> So let come what may, what ever it is, I only
>   say
> That I have Christ in my heart, I have
>   Christ in my heart.

Do you know your life is in God's hands? Can you leave the outcome of your circumstances in His care? Are you ready to turn over your greatest wor-ries and fears to Him? Have you prayed, "The Lord's will be done"? Like Esther, are you prepared to say, "The worst that can happen is that I lose my life on earth and join my Father in heaven. But I will fearlessly press on into His will, and if I perish, I perish"?

In Acts 21, Paul was making his way to Jerusalem when he came to Caesarea to visit with believers who lived and ministered there. A prophet arrived from Judea, took Paul's sash, tied himself with it, and announced, *"So shall the Jews at Jerusalem bind the man that owns this belt, and deliver him into the hands of the Gentiles" (Acts 21:11).* Paul's friends began begging him to cancel his trip to Jerusalem, but he responded, *"What do you mean by weeping and breaking my heart? For I am ready not only to be bound, but also to die at Jerusalem for the name of the Lord Jesus" (Acts 21:13).* In the previous chapter, Paul made another clear statement about his attitude: *"But none of these things move me; nor do I count my life dear to myself, so that I may finish my race with joy" (Acts 20:24).*

Paul's outlook on life was simple: *For to me, to live is Christ, and to die is gain (Phil. 1:21).* He actually had mixed emotions because leaving this world to be with Christ was a "far better" proposition for him, yet he felt it was necessary to remain on earth awhile longer for the benefit of the Philippians (see Phil. 1:23-24). Paul was unstoppable because nothing frightened him; he considered, *none of us lives to himself, and no one dies to himself. If we live, we live, to the Lord; and if we die, we die to the Lord. Therefore, whether we live or die, we are the Lord's (Rom. 14:7-8).* How can you harm a man like that? A man who says, "Let them kill me; if I perish, I perish. Then I'll be with the Lord in His eternal kingdom." He was undaunted, because God held his future.

Do you trust God for your eternal destiny? Do you believe He will receive you into heaven when you die? Does it seem inconsistent to trust Him with your eternal future, but act like you cannot trust Him for tomorrow? Which is the greater concern, tomorrow or the eternal stretch of time that lies beyond the grave? If you trust Him for eternity, then trust Him for tomorrow.

What are you anxious about today? What do you fear? What worries you? Would you be willing to hand over all those issues to God right now? God would be pleased if you would trust Him enough to cast *all your care upon him; for he careth for you (1 Pet. 5:7, KJV; see also Phil. 4:6-7)*. You have been carrying around a heavy burden, and God wants you to come to Him and say, "OK, Lord, I've carried it as far as I can, You can take it from here. Work this out according to your purpose, because You know what is best and Your work is flawless. I'm through worrying about it because I've given my worries to You."

Let me make a suggestion I think will help you leave your worries and fears with God. Rather than begging Him over and over to take your worries, start thanking Him for His help, and for His promise that *He who has begun a good work in you will complete it until the day of Jesus Christ (Phil. 1:6)*. Start saying, "Thank You, Lord, for watching over me, for providing all I need, for taking care of the problems that have driven me crazy." You have His promises, so if you embrace them in faith and thank God for being true to His Word, then you will be walking in faith, for *faith is the substance of things hoped for, the evidence of things not seen (Heb. 11:1)*.

Reflecting on Abraham's faith, Paul observed that

he *did not waver at the promise of God through unbelief, but was strengthened in faith, giving glory to God (Rom. 4:20).* He was already praising God for a future that was only a promise, and he thanked God before he had any evidence of fulfillment. We have the Word of a God who is faithful, a God who keeps His promises. Even though we have no idea how God will deliver us or see us through the hard times, we can still learn to thank Him because we have a promise. This is faith, and it is the kind of faith that dispels fear.

You can trust God, because He made you dependent on Him and gave you the ability to trust Him the way a baby rests peacefully in the arms of his or her mother. The moment you surrender to God in trust, the moment you pray—"Well, OK, Lord, my life, my things, my family—all of it! It is all Yours, and if I perish, I perish"—you will enter His rest and find His peace deep within your soul. From that deep place you will say, "Lord, I realize now how much You love me. And, Father, I love You. From now on, that is all that matters. However You want to take care of my life is fine with me. I trust You because You are my Father and I'm Your child."

Prayer

Father, how great is the love You have given to us,
that we should be called the children of God.
As Your children,
we are able to gather up the issues of life that are
troubling,
generate anxiety,

manufacture illusory fears,
and throw them over to You,
knowing that You care for us.
Lord God,
set people free;
from worry, fear, anxiety,
and the millions of unnecessary concerns about
tomorrow.
Give us grace to be aware of all You have done;
and respond with thanksgiving.
Give us a glimpse of all that You still have planned
for us,
so we can plunge into the future rejoicing.
Now we commit our ways fully unto You,
trusting You to work out Your eternal purpose and plan
in and through our lives,
through Jesus Christ our Lord and Savior.
Amen.

CHAPTER 2

Count It All Joy

My brethren, count it all joy when you fall into various trials, knowing that the testing of your faith produces patience.

(James 1:2-3)

ANCIENT HEROES

Abraham

Let's take a walk through the ancient Middle East for a brief visit with three people. Our first encounter is with Abraham, who has the distinction of being known as the father of our faith and the *friend of God (Gen. 18:17)*.

The theme of Abraham's story is promise. God asked Abraham to leave his family and join Him on an adventure. He spoke of a bright future, a fertile land, and a nation that would bless all families of the earth. The central promise on which all the other good things depended was the birth of a son. This promise, however, was outrageous, because Abraham was an old man and his wife was infertile. Nevertheless, God was true to His word, and Isaac was born to Abraham and Sarah. Imagine how the old man must have doted on his miracle baby.

But when Isaac reached manhood, God *tested Abraham*, and said, *"Take now your son, your only son Isaac, whom you love, and go to the land of Moriah, and offer him there as a burnt offering on one of the mountains of which I shall tell you"* (Gen. 22:1-2). The first time the word *love* appears in the Bible is in this incredibly strange context. God asked Abraham to take what he loved most and place him on an altar.

In telling this part of Abraham's story, the Book of Genesis repeatedly uses the word *and* to join one sentence to the next. The name for this literary device—when connector words like *but* or *and* are used repeatedly in a paragraph—is *polysyndeton*. Writers use polysyndeton for different reasons; sometimes to create rhythm, to slow down the pace of a passage, and other times to cause the reader to feel the flow of a continuous action, as if one event is pressing its way into another *and* another *and* another.

The feeling we get with all these *ands* is forward momentum, as if the whole episode is rushing along until Isaac's body is burning on the altar at Mount Moriah. We also have an uneasy feeling that God would require this from Abraham, and that Abraham would willingly comply with such an outlandish demand. It seems Abraham set out on this *journey of obedience* without hesitation.*

Fortunately, we were told at the beginning of this

---

* See Leonard Sweet for a "hidden school of interpretation" regarding this event that is different from what we usually hear. *Out of the Question . . . Into the Mystery* (Colorado Springs, CO: Waterbrook Press, 2004), 49-61.

story that *God tested Abraham,* so we know the under-lying meaning of these events. Abraham believed God when He promised him not only a son but also so many descendants they would become as innumer-able as the stars (see Gen. 15:4-6). Now Abraham's faith and loyalty to God were being tested. Because Abraham's devotion to God was unshakable, he passed the test and proved his reverence for God (see Gen. 22:10-12). God never intended for Abraham to go through with the sacrifice, but He arranged this exer-cise to expose the strengths and weaknesses of Abra-ham's commitment to God.

MOSES

The second person we meet is Moses. This great leader, prophet, and law-giver stood before the chil-dren of Israel at the end of his life and explained to them the meaning of their hardships in the desert: *"And you shall remember that the Lord your God led you all the way these forty years in the wilderness, to humble you and test you, to know what was in your heart, whether you would keep His commandments or not"(Deut. 8:2).* Did God really learn anything by testing Abraham or the people of Israel? No! God had always known what lay in the human heart (see 1 Kin. 8:39). God tested them so they could discover the truth about themselves. In Jeremiah 17:9-10, after God said, *"The heart is deceitful above all things, And desperately wicked; Who can know it?"* He answered, *"I, the LORD, search the heart, I test the mind."* God's people need to be shown the truth about their spiritual condition; God already knows.

When Moses climbed Mount Sinai to receive God's law, the people of Israel promised, *"All that the Lord has spoken we will do" (Ex. 19:8).* Unfortunately, this wonderful pledge was much easier on paper. God later acknowledged they were "right in all that they have spoken"; that is, they used the right words, they had the right vocabulary. But what about follow through?

"Oh, that they had such a heart in them that they would fear Me and always keep all My commandments, that it might be well with them and with their children forever!" (Deut. 5:29). They had the words, but not the heart (see also Matt. 21:28-32). That is why the human heart has to be tested because our hearts can deceive us, but they cannot deceive God. He wants our true devotion.

JOB

Our third visit is in the home of Job, a man God allowed to be tested severely. Loss of property and income, of family and friends, and finally the loss of health and peace drove Job into a dark pit of pain and suffering. But Job never cursed or denied God, never betrayed his integrity, and never stopped believing God was his only hope. Apparently Job had at least a glimmer of an idea of a divine intention behind his ordeal, because he said, *"When He has tested me, I shall come forth as gold" (Job 23:10).* Job did so well that he became an heroic example of *perseverance* (James 5:11). If we connect Job's perseverance mentioned in James 5 to the perseverance of James 1 (the only other time James mentions *perseverance*), then we begin to see the significance and purpose of our various trials and tests.

CHRISTIANS WHO TALK THE WALK

While meditating on the first two verses of James and the *testing of our faith,* I was privileged to join our junior high school summer camp in the mountains near Big Bear. On our third night together, we sat around the campfire, and I told about Jesus' invitation to would-be disciples; they were to deny themselves, take up their cross, and follow Him (see Matt. 16:24; Mark 8:34; Luke 9:23). We discussed what it would mean for them to make a total commitment to God. I also told them about the commitment I had made to God more than 50 years ago at a summer camp, and what it still meant to me today.

I announced to them, "I want to reaffirm my commitment to God; who wants to join me?" Instantly a few kids stood to their feet, then more and more, until everyone present was standing. I encouraged them to think for themselves, examine their hearts, and answer the question, "Why am I standing?" If we stand only because everyone else stands, we are likely to fall under the pressure of a different crowd.

Some of the kids wanted to stay by the fire that evening singing, praying, and spending more time with Jesus, so we gave them that option. However, the majority of the campers found the snack bar, game room, and basketball courts more appealing than worship time around the campfire, despite the fact a few minutes earlier we had declared together, "We will deny ourselves and follow Jesus." Of course, we expect this sort of fickleness from children, whose attention span flits with the speed of a hummingbird from one activity to another. But adult Christians who have a hard time matching what they say at church with what they do in their everyday lives need not wonder why God puts them through various trials to test them.

When James mentions *various trials,* he uses a Greek word that means *to scrutinize* or *prove.* Suppose you wanted to have someone reupholster your car seats, but you are worried that the thread they use is not strong enough. How can you prove the strength of the thread? By testing it, by stretching it between two powerful and opposing forces. The strength of the thread is revealed by the amount of force it can resist without breaking or how long it is able to withstand the test. In a similar way, God reveals our faith and love by stretching us with our daily trials and tests. In effect, God says, "You say you trust Me, but do you know the strength of your trust? Will it be there when you need it? Will your trust remain strong when you have no idea where I am or what I am doing? We will test your faith to discover its strengths, its flaws, and to learn where it still needs to mature."

Christians and non-Christians alike tend to engage in a certain amount of self-deception. We sing of our love for God, we tell Him we love Him, and we truly believe we love Him, but we might not know the strength of our love and whether it can *endure all things (1 Cor. 13:7).* Like the people of Israel, I may say the right words, but not back them up with my actions. So our love for the Lord—its genuineness, strength, and depth—has to be put to the test.

One of the concerns James repeatedly addresses in his letter is the human tendency to separate words from actions. In chapter two, he addresses Christians who do nothing more than say, *"Depart in peace, be warmed and filled"* to *"a brother or sister"* who is *"naked and destitute of daily food"* (James 2:15-16). We are not helping anyone when we give them words rather than tangible help. The apostle John had this same idea in mind when he told believers who had food and clothing to spare but failed to share those things with others. *My little children, let us not love in word or in tongue, but in deed and in truth* (1 John 3:17-18). In this context, words are cheap. In the same way that our love for others can be cheapened, so can our love for God. We can say, "I love You, God" so many times we convince ourselves our words are true. But if our love is never externalized, never expressed in a tangible action, then we are deceiving ourselves (see 1 John 4:20).

JOY? GET REAL!

The Book of James begins with an imperative (or command), *Count it all joy when you fall into various trials.* He seems to be saying, "When trouble and hardship invade your life, interpret these intrusions as *joyful* events." My initial reaction to this command is, "Get real!" To welcome trouble with open arms is not only difficult, but totally illogical. If that is what James is telling believers to do, I have to admit I cannot com-

ply. I do not enjoy taking tests, and I am especially ad-
verse to flunking tests—because that means *repeating*
the test! At face value, James' advice seems absurd.
Nevertheless, he tells us to adopt this strange attitude
to life's unpleasant circumstances. How is that possible?

Jesus' teaching in the Sermon on the Mount does
not improve our discomfort with the command to
count it all joy when we are tested and tried. For example, Jesus said, *"Blessed are those who are persecuted
for righteousness' sake, For theirs is the kingdom of heaven"*
(Matt. 5:10). Jesus used the word *blessed* as a teaching
device common in His time. We could also translate
this verse as: "Oh, the happiness you have when persecuted for righteousness sake . . . Oh, the happiness
you have when you are reviled and persecuted, and
they say all kinds of evil against you falsely for My
sake. Rejoice and be exceedingly glad." Is this a difficult command to obey? No, it is impossible!

When the prophet Jeremiah was persecuted for
speaking on God's behalf, he did not rejoice! *"Then I
said, 'I will not make mention of Him, Nor speak anymore
in His name'"* *(Jer. 20:9).* Our reaction to persecution
and rejection is generally closer to Jeremiah's than either Jesus' or James' teaching. If you were ridiculed by
someone at work, school, or in your neighborhood because you were a Christian, how likely is it that your
first response would be, "What a delightful experience! I'm so happy to be treated like an idiot"? We
must admit that rejoicing in the face of trouble or
ridicule is not a natural response.

Luke recorded Jesus' words on rejoicing in the face

of persecution, but with a slightly different accent: *Blessed are you when men hate you, And when they exclude you, And revile you, and cast out your name as evil, For the Son of Man's sake (Luke 6:22).*

On this occasion, Jesus went so far as to say, "Rejoice in that day and leap for joy!" Does it not seem like He has gone too far? *Leap for joy?*

Why would we want to rejoice and leap for joy when mistreated for Jesus' sake? Well, the Lord provided two reasons: First, *For indeed your reward is great in heaven (Luke 6:23).* I have discovered when my belief in Christ creates problems for me, meditating on the fact that I have a reward in heaven gives me the perspective I need to accept my circumstances and even rejoice in them. So we do not rejoice because people hate and exclude us or trash our reputation, but because the Lord promised, *"great is your reward in heaven."* Do you see how it is possible to take Jesus at His word and say, "Oh man, I've got it so good. I'm going to spend eternity with my Lord! What a great reward." *We do not lose heart* as Paul said, because *our light affliction, which is but for a moment, is working for us a far more exceeding and eternal weight of glory (2 Cor. 4:16-17).* Our hardship is *light* and lasts only *a moment*, while our future glory is an excessive weight and will last for eternity. As Paul told the Romans, *I consider that the sufferings of this present time are not worthy to be compared with the glory which shall be revealed in us (Rom. 8:18).*

The second reason Jesus gave is that *in like manner their fathers did to the prophets (Luke 6:23).* In other words, this unique and respected class of spiritually-gifted individuals known as God's prophets suffered the same kind of treatment. You are in good company. If you suffer because of your faith in Christ, for standing with Him against popular opinion, for loving the outcasts and sinners as He did, then you can be sure you stand in a long line of godly heroes who suffered the same kind of treatment—and even worse.

The heroic martyr, Stephen, made a revealing observation about the Old Testament prophets. Before we look at his statement, consider his entire speech he delivered to the ruling religious council of Israel. Stephen emphasized Israel had a history of disobeying God, turning on His messengers, and rejecting His Word. But the way Stephen structured his speech also revealed a pattern of initial rejection followed by salvation. For example, Joseph was rejected by his brothers, then later saved them and the rest of his family (see Acts 7:9-15). The same pattern is repeated about Moses who was rejected by the Hebrews, then returned to rule and save his people (see Acts 7:23-36). In the same way, men of the council were *betrayers and murderers* of Jesus, *the Just One,* who would be recognized in His second coming as their rightful Ruler and Savior *(Acts 7:51-56, KJV).*

In this well-crafted speech, Stephen asked, *"Which of the prophets did your fathers not persecute?" (Acts 7:52).* He challenged them to name one prophet their ancestors had not abused or killed. They proved themselves to be the true sons of their fathers by murdering the One whose coming all the prophets had foretold. At this point, his audience became so enraged they dragged Stephen outside the city and stoned him to death. But before he was taken from the court, he had a vision of Jesus Christ standing at God's right hand. Stephen was in the company of the prophets, the company of Jesus, and heaven opened to him.

"You are in good company," Jesus said, "if people abuse or reject you for My sake." In fact, *Woe to you when all men speak well of you, For so did their fathers to the false prophets" (Luke 6:26).* If you are winning popularity contests in a culture that glorifies violence, celebrates moral corruption, oppresses the poor, is obsessed with greed, and indulges itself in luxury while the rest of the world suffers, then something is wrong with your character. Jesus said we are supposed to be *salt (Matt. 5:13).* Salt on a cut or scratch hurts, even though it may help fight off infection. The world is covered with open wounds, and if our presence does not *sting* enough to get a reaction, then it is possible we have lost our saltiness.

At this point you may be thinking, "OK, Chuck, I see where you're going with this. But there's one big problem in what you've said so far, and that has to do with the *source* of our suffering. I admit, there's plenty of trouble and hardship in my life, even some grief. But my suffering is *random*, the 'luck of the draw,' as they say. I did not get sick, laid off, lose my spouse, become injured because of Jesus' sake. Cancer isn't a form of persecution. So I can't look on my circumstances joyfully because I don't see any purpose to my suffering. It's just some kind of *misfortune*. After all, I am no Abraham, Moses, or Job!"

Or you can go a step further and say, "I cannot accept my trials joyfully because I deserve what I'm going through. I sinned, and now I am facing the consequences of my sin. God can't get any glory through the pain I'm in now, and I can't hope to improve my life because of this suffering." But you have forgotten a very important truth. Do not beat yourself up for forgetting because it seems other believers as far back as the New Testament have also had similar memory lapses, *And you have forgotten the exhortation which speaks to you as to sons: . . . For whom the Lord loves He chastens (Heb. 12:5-6)*. We learn some of our most valuable lessons through the suffering we bring on ourselves. Once disciplined—education through correction—we are trained to live a better life for Christ.

No doubt a difference exists between suffering as persecution, suffering as punishment, and the normal suffering that comes to humans in a fallen world. But what is critical in all suffering is not where it came from, but how you respond when you fall into *various trials*, as James said. In fact, the Greek word *various (poikilois)* means variegated color, so the suffering can come in all forms and for a variety of reasons. Whether a *thorn in the flesh (2 Cor. 12:7)*, suffering *for doing good (1 Pet. 3:17)*, or simply experiencing the aches and pains *common to man (1 Cor. 10:13), we know that all things work together for good to those who love God, to those who are the called according to His purpose (Rom. 8:28)*. God can work our troubles into a configuration that fits *His purpose*. We will not stress the distinction between the various trials we fall into but look for reasons to *count it all joy* when we do fall into them.

THE APOSTLES AND THE IMPOSSIBLE

Our church provides a prayer hotline for people in crisis. Sadly, callers have told our pastors, "You don't know what my life is like. You don't know what I have been dealing with for the last year. I just can't do this anymore." They call to tell someone they are ready to give up their faith and resign from their walk with the Lord. These people do not believe it is possible to endure the trying of their faith, let alone *count it all joy.*

Do we know of Christians who have been able to rejoice in their suffering? Well, yes we do, as a matter of fact. When the apostles were imprisoned and then beaten, they *departed from the presence of the council [that abused them], rejoicing that they were counted worthy to suffer shame for His name (Acts 5:41).* The apostles proved it is not impossible to do as Jesus said, to *rejoice* when mistreated for His name. But we need some clarification because, like we saw earlier, rejoicing in the face of trouble or ridicule is not logical, natural, or even possible. So why were the apostles able to rejoice when they were beaten?

The word *natural* is a giveaway. On our own and of ourselves, we cannot *count it all joy when we fall into various trials.* But God is able to perform a work in us that we could never perform for ourselves because what is impossible for us is *not with God; for with God all things are possible (Mark 10:27).* Jesus told us to rejoice in the face of persecution and the apostles proved it to be possible, but only because they had experienced God's work in them, enabling them to do what was otherwise impossible.

Here is a New Testament guarantee for you to hang on to: God is faithful. This means He will not demand of you anything He will not enable you to perform (see Phil. 2:12-13; 1 Thess. 5:23). The Scriptures give many examples of God commanding ordinary people to perform impossible tasks. He commanded Noah to float hundreds of animals to safety through the flood, Moses to lead the Hebrew slaves out of Egypt, and Gideon to liberate Israel from the Midianites. Jesus told a paralyzed man to walk, a bent over woman to stand up straight, a man with a withered hand to stretch it out, and a dead man to rise! So when Jesus tells you and me to *rejoice* when persecuted and *glory in tribulations (Rom. 5:3),* He will also give us the ability to do the impossible. If you are willing to obey God, then He will make certain you have the capacity to do what He demands.

I will tell you a mystery: If you say "yes" to God, if you say, "I *will* count it all joy when I fall into various trials" and adopt that attitude, then an unspeakable joy will flood your soul. You will find yourself rejoicing because of the irrepressible joy you feel. God will give you the joy to make your rejoicing real. Your attitude will change from the inside.

Paul complained to God about a *thorn in his flesh* and asked Him repeatedly to remove it. But each time he prayed, God answered, *"My grace is sufficient for you, for My strength is made perfect in weakness."* How did Paul respond to that revelation? *Therefore most gladly I will rather boast in my infirmities, that the power of Christ may rest upon me. . . . For when I am weak, then I am strong (2 Cor. 12:9-10).* Paul was able to tell the

Philippians, *Yes, and if I am being poured out as a drink offering on the sacrifice and service of your faith, I am glad and rejoice with you all (Phil. 2:17).*

Turning to other New Testament writers, we find the following quote in the Book of Hebrews: *for you had compassion on me in my chains, and joyfully accepted the plundering of your goods, knowing that you have a better and an enduring possession for yourselves in heaven (Heb. 10:34).* These believers had the attitude of heavenly citizens who could say, "Ha! You plundered my possessions, but I have a heavenly home that you cannot break into and enter, and a reward that cannot be taken away." No one can touch what God has laid up for us in heaven. With our eyes set on eternal things, we can rejoice in the loss of temporal things.

Consider also the testimonial of Peter who spoke of God's power to keep us in Him. He observed:

> In this you greatly rejoice, though now for a
> little while, if need be, you have been
> grieved by various trials, that the
> genuineness of your faith, being much more
> precious than gold that perishes, though it is
> tested by fire, may be found to praise,
> honor, and glory at the revelation of Jesus
> Christ, whom having not seen you love.
> Though now you do not see Him, yet
> believing, you rejoice with joy inexpressible
> and full of glory.
>
> (1 Pet. 1:6-8)

Jesus told us to rejoice when persecuted, Paul said our future glory will more than compensate for our current suffering, and James told us to count it all joy when we fall into various trials; the apostles did this very thing. Therefore, rejoicing in our hardship and suffering *is* possible after all.

We have seen it is possible to adopt a joyful perspective when we fall into various trials when we understand the nature of God's tests. We realize we are in good company, we know that all things work for God, and that God has laid aside for us a great reward in heaven. If we move on to the next verse in James, we will find another reason to *count it all joy: Knowing that the testing of your faith produces patience (James 1:3).*

GIVE ME PATIENCE, NOW!

"Patience is a virtue"—one I desperately need and desire. God did not make me a patient person by nature. Many times my impatience has rewarded me nothing but trouble because I was unwilling to wait on God and I ran ahead of Him. When God allows stressful circumstances to test me, I will usually start out well enough, praying and looking to Him for help. But then I get impatient while waiting for God to do something, and I decide to take matters into my own hands, take some kind of action, and try to bring resolution to my problem. Perhaps what I feel is the same frustration that drove Abraham and Sarah to use Hagar as a surrogate mother or rushed King Saul into presenting God a sacrifice he had no business offering. If God seems to be moving too slowly for me, I assume He needs me to help Him along. My lack of patience, however, almost always results in me making a total mess of my situation. I am gradually learning from God that I must wait on Him to accomplish His work in me.

How wonderful it would be if patience came in a pill! Or if it were one of those miraculous gifts of the Spirit. Or if God instantly gave patience to anyone who asked. In the New Testament you can find lists of gifts of the Spirit, but you will not find patience on any of those lists. We do not become patient miraculously or instantly, nor is there a patience pill. Rather, as Paul said in Romans 5:3, *"Tribulation produces patience"* (or endurance or perseverance). James said, *"The testing of your faith produces patience"* (James 1:3).

One reason why we find it difficult to be patient is the illusion that while we wait for God, nothing is happening, but that's not usually the case. Think about a visit to the doctor. When we find ourselves sitting in the waiting room of a doctor's office, we feel nothing is happening, so we distract ourselves from the boredom of our inactivity. Because nothing is happening *to* us, we feel as if nothing is happening *for* us. Yet the truth is that a lot is going on that we can't see or be part of, some of which is for our benefit. While we wait on God, He's working around us and within us, preparing us for our circumstances and our circumstances for us. One of the works He performs in us is to develop patience and endurance, because once these qualities are operative, virtue and victory can follow.

The way God leads our lives and solves our

problems is always best because we belong to a God who loves us as His children and who is perfecting His eternal work in our lives. The great 19th century preacher Charles Spurgeon once said that if we were as wise as God, we would choose our trials for ourselves. Whatever God wants to do in our lives is better than the best outcome we could imagine. So waiting on Him as we go through our trials is the wisest course of action we can take. If we attempt to dodge or escape the tests He sends or we try to rush through them in our impatience, then we forfeit the work God desires to do for us and in us.

PREPARED FOR GOD'S EXAM

Do you know anyone who does not love the brash disciple Peter? What a great heart he demonstrated in his devotion to Jesus. I think Peter meant every word when he promised Jesus he would never desert Him (see Mark 14:27-29). Peter was convinced his love and commitment to Jesus were so strong, that nothing could break him. When Jesus told Peter before the rooster announced the dawn he would deny Him, this disciple *spoke more vehemently, "If I have to die with You, I will not deny You!" (Mark 14:31).* Then Peter was put to the test.

Now as Peter was below in the courtyard, one of the servant girls of the high priest came. And when she saw Peter warming himself, she looked at him and said, "You also were with Jesus of Nazareth."

But he denied it, saying, "I neither know nor understand

what you are saying." And he went out onto the porch, and a rooster crowed (Mark 14:66-67).

That was Peter's first strike. Two more would follow as Peter denied Jesus with the same vehemence with which he had vowed he would never deny Him. Then the rooster crowed a second time, and *Peter called to mind the word that Jesus had said to him, "Before the rooster crows twice, you will deny Me three times." And when he thought about it, he wept (Mark 14:71-72).*

Not long after Jesus' resurrection, Peter was dragged before the very council that had condemned Jesus to face interrogation regarding a crippled man suddenly healed at the disciple's command. The council asked Peter, *"By what power or by what name have you done this?" (Acts 4:7).* Remember, Peter had been afraid to admit he knew Jesus when the Lord was on trial before these religious leaders. But Luke says:

> Then Peter, filled with the Holy Spirit, said to them, "Rulers of the people and elders of Israel: If we this day are judged for a good deed done to the helpless man, by what means he has been made well, let it be known to you all, and to all the people of Israel, that by the name of Jesus Christ of Nazareth, whom you crucified, whom God raised from the dead, by Him this man stands here before you whole."
>
> (Acts 4:8-10)

Peter took a great risk! Can this be the same man who swore he did not know Jesus? Yes, he is the same man, but it was after a radical change; Peter was now *filled with the Holy Spirit.*

What I find impossible because of the weakness of my human nature—despite my resolve, willpower, self-discipline, and sincere longing—God makes possible by His Spirit. Before Jesus bid the disciples farewell and ascended into heaven, He told them, *"But you shall receive power when the Holy Spirit has come upon you; and you shall be witnesses to Me in Jerusalem, and in all Judea and Samaria, and to the end of the earth" (Acts 1:8).* I long so much to be an authentic witness for Jesus, to have people point at me and say, "He is a Christian whose life is a reflection of Jesus Christ." But I am not that person because my human nature is not capable of copying Jesus. Like Peter, I can imagine Jesus saying to me, *"The spirit indeed is willing, but the flesh is weak"* (Matt. 26:41).

The weakness of my human nature, however, is not the last word on what I can and cannot be in God's kingdom. If I recognize my own inadequacy, I also recognize the power of God's Spirit as He works within me. *I can do all things* through His help and through the grace of the Lord Jesus *who strengthens me (Phil. 4:13).* I can pass the test, not merely in words or slogans by which I talk about love and commitment, but by a living demonstration of hope, trust, and endurance.

Do you remember Daniel's three friends in Babylon? King Nebuchadnezzar had a huge golden statue *built in the plain of Dura, in the province of Babylon, (Dan. 3:1)* and demanded that all court officials and international dignitaries in Babylon come to its dedication.

They were commanded to bow before the gold image. But Shadrach, Meshach, and Abed-Nego refused to bow and for that crime were bound and thrown into the *midst of the burning fiery furnace (Dan. 3:6)*. Watching them from a safe distance, the king noticed instead of being burned to death, they were walking around and a fourth person had joined them. When he commanded them to exit the furnace, they were unscathed.

Reading this story, we come to a painful realization: God did not protect these three brave men from the fire, but he delivered them *in* the fire. We would love for God to protect us from life's trials, but that is not His way; we are no better if our path is strewn with roses. We learn lessons from stepping on thorns, but even then we are not alone. God delivers us as we walk on through the test.

THAT YOU MAY BE PERFECT

A few years ago, a young man who was an aspiring actor in Hollywood attended our church. One of his first big opportunities came when he was offered a leading role in a new television series. But when he read a sample script and noticed that the general drift of the series was rather raunchy, he refused the contract. His agent was livid and warned him, "If you turn down this offer, you'll never get another chance at anything! You're throwing away your career." The actor, however, had made up his mind. No matter what it cost him, he would not sacrifice his integrity.

Unfortunately, the young man had not worked in

awhile and was beginning to worry about how he would make rent. When his phone rang and a producer invited him to a film shoot in Cabo San Lucas, he immediately got excited, believing this was God's answer to his prayers. But then the producer explained, "We are filming a movie based on marlin fishing in the Baja Sweepstakes in the Gulf of Mexico. We can't pay you anything because of our shoestring budget, but we're willing to offer you a contract for a share of the profits if the film sells. So, do you want to go fishing?" Not having any other prospects, he joined the film crew, which wrapped up their project one day before the contest ended. The actor decided to enter the contest that last day, and he ended up catching the largest marlin and winning a grand prize of $240,000.

Like many other couples, Kay and I have been hit hard by financial problems, especially in the first 25 years of our marriage. We have always believed *God would supply all our needs according to His riches in glory by Christ Jesus (Phil. 4:19),* and I am happy to say this is one area of my life where I have passed the test and found God faithful. But that does not mean going through the fire is a pleasant experience. Nevertheless, once we discovered the wonderful ways God proved to be with us through those trials, we began to greet them as new adventures and learned to *count it all joy* when the financial pressure came.

If you put your trust in God, then expect Him to test your faith, hope, and love. Once you have made the decision to *rejoice in the Lord always* and give thanks for everything *(Phil. 4:4, 6),* do your best not to flip-flop between faith and doubt. You know what I mean; one minute you are saying, "God, my circumstances are in Your hands. I will trust You alone." Then the next minute you are saying, "Oh dear, what am I going to do?" When the stress builds to the point you can no longer take it, you throw the whole thing in God's lap again, but quickly take it back through worry. James addressed this very problem when he said, *But let him ask in faith, with no doubting, for he who doubts is like a wave of the sea driven and tossed by the wind (James 1:6).*

I have found it helpful to remind myself in adversity that it is only a test. In fact, now when I am at the point I begin to feel disturbed, I take it as a signal to remind myself, "This is a test." With that realization, I am instantly blessed with a new perspective. I am then able to say, "By God's grace and the power of the Holy Spirit, I will pass this test. I will wait on God for the best outcome which He has already designed and guarantees. I will not take this problem back into my own hands through worry." God then works patience into my life, and through patience, *every good gift and every perfect gift (James 1:17).*

But may the God of all grace, who called us to His eternal glory by Christ Jesus, after you have suffered a while, perfect, establish, strengthen, and settle you. To Him be the glory and the dominion forever and ever. Amen (1 Pet. 5:10-11).

Prayer

Father, we thank You for the infinite love
that puts our faith to the test,
disciplines us as Your children,
and works all things together for our good.

But help us, Lord, to rejoice when we fall into
various trials;
knowing You are working in us,
exposing areas of weakness, deception, and
false confidence.
We are constantly learning about our complete
dependence on You.
Help us wait patiently upon You so that we might see
Your perfect work,
and seeing Your work, rejoice in Your victory.
In Jesus' name.
Amen.

CHAPTER 3

Do Your Best and Commit the Rest

When Joab saw that the battle line was against him before and behind, he chose some of Israel's best, and put them in battle array against the Syrians. And the rest of the people he put under the command of Abishai his brother, and they set themselves in battle array against the people of Ammon. Then he said, "If the Syrians are too strong for me, then you shall help me; but if the people of Ammon are too strong for you, then I will help you. Be of good courage, and let us be strong for our people and for the cities of our God. And may the Lord do what is good in His sight."

(1 Chr. 19:10-13)

GOOD COURAGE

A sinister mood hovers over the story of King David and Hanun, the neighboring Ammonite king. The opening sentence explains, *It happened after this that*

Nahash the king of the people of Ammon died (1 Chr. 19:1).
I have always felt Nahash—pronounced *Nawh-kawsh*—was a creepy name. In fact, his name is related
to the hissing sound snakes make; in a slightly differ-
ent form it is translated *serpent (Gen. 3:1).* Nahash appeared in the story of King Saul when he attacked
Jabesh Gilead and threatened to gouge out the right
eyes of everyone in the city. He intended to insult all
of Israel by this gruesome act of mutilation (see 1 Sam.
11:1-2). The people did not have fond memories regarding the Ammonites, so beginning with a reminder of Hanun's father, the storyteller is letting us
know in advance there is trouble ahead.

We are a little surprised David would want to offer
condolences to the crown prince of Ammon after his
father died, but in the parallel version of the story in
2 Samuel, David makes reference to the *kindness* Nahash had shown him in some unrecorded incident
(see 2 Sam. 10:2). We can imagine having been defeated by King Saul, Nahash would be eager to support David whom he may have perceived as Saul's enemy. Still we would wonder if this attempt at
improving foreign relations would not in some way
jeopardize national policy, and why David would
make this conciliatory gesture. Perhaps the meaning
of Hanun's name—*willingness to show favor*—sounded
promising to David, who preferred making peace
through diplomacy rather than warfare.

The reputation of David's unbeatable military ma-
chine preceded his envoys and raised suspicion of Hanun's advisers, *"Do you think that David really honors
your father because he has sent comforters to you? Did his*

servants not come to you to search out and overthrow and spy out the land?" (v. 3). Then Hanun did something that seems characteristic of his father. He insulted David and Israel by humiliating and performing a symbolic mutilation of the delegation sent to the Ammonites. He had their beards shaved and their clothing cut so they were exposed to public shame.

When David was told what happened, he sent word to his envoy to take temporary residence in the desert city of Jericho until their beards had grown back. But even then, there is no indication he was ready to declare war on Hanun. Israel had a command from God not to harass the Ammonites when they passed near their territory on their journey through the wilderness (see Deut. 2:19). Hanun, however, panicked when he realized he had offended David, so he hired Syrian mercenaries along with chariots and horsemen to engage Israel in battle, which forced David to send his armies out under Joab's command.

In the warfare of the ancient Middle East, two situations almost always proved fatal: First, if an army panicked and ran from their enemies. This would expose their backs to their attackers. Panic usually resulted in the ruthless slaughter of the fleeing army. The second serious threat was being surrounded by the enemy. Soldiers caught in the crossfire of two flanks, before and behind them, had no hope of escape and their backs were always exposed. Once Joab marched up to the Ammonites who had positioned themselves in front of the gates of their city, and the Syrians moved in from the fields behind him, he realized he and his forces were trapped. But Joab did not panic. He took command of his shock troops and prepared them to attack the Syrians, who were the stronger force. He gave his brother, Abishai, the remainder of the army and set them against the Ammonites.

When the children of Israel had come through the wilderness and stood at the border of the Promised Land, Moses addressed them one last time, *Be strong and of good courage, do not fear nor be afraid of them; for the Lord your God, He is the One who goes with you. He will not leave you nor forsake you (Deut. 31:6).* These words became God's motto for Israel regarding any national threat. Joab drew on this promise in the critical moments before clashing swords with the enemy. He told his brother Abishai and all the other soldiers, "Be courageous, be valiant, and we'll leave the consequences with the Lord. Let Him do whatever pleases Him. We'll give this battle our best effort and leave the results to God" (see 2 Sam. 10:9-12).

God never requires or expects from you more than what you are capable of doing. You may not be the most qualified applicant for the job God has at hand; your best may not be as good as someone else's, but if you do what you can, then God will be pleased. God does not need us to be the absolute best candidate because He is wise and strong enough to get the job done. He does not mind using foolish things to shame the wise or weak things to shame the mighty. He does not want anyone boasting in His presence (see 1 Cor. 1:26-31); His grace compensates for our infirmities and weaknesses (see 2 Cor. 12:9-10). All God asks of us is courage, diligence, and to do what we can.

Sometimes we make up excuses to weasel our way

out of God's service because we are overwhelmed with our own sense of inadequacy. Other people are obviously more qualified for the work God has called us to do, and they could do a better job. But God has not called us to do any work to perfection; He only asks us to do what we can. If you can be brave, put your confidence in God, plunge into His will, then you can be sure He will bring about the results He desires and use your life in the process.

We find a wonderful story in Jesus' life about a woman who poured very expensive oil over His head while He sat at a meal with His disciples. Immediately the disciples criticized the woman, and they seemed to hold Jesus responsible because there was no call for her to be doing this to Him; it seemed like a waste of oil. Jesus, however, defended her, explained her actions, and said, *"She has done what she could"* (Mark 14:8). Is that not a beautiful phrase? Restricted by her culture, a woman could not do much to show someone of Jesus' status and honor how much she loved and adored Him. She could not pray with Him in the Garden of Gethsemane, she could not stand up for Him at His trial, nor could she rescue Him from the cross. But she did what she could, and for Jesus, that was enough. He promised that wherever the gospel would be preached around the world, the message of what that woman did would also be celebrated *"as a memorial to her"* (Mark 14:9).

ACTIVE TRUST

One of my mottos for life is, "Do your best, commit the rest." I have known believers who say they trust in

God. The truth is they are lazy or apathetic. Our trust in God is not an excuse for not giving God our best effort. Joab left the outcome of the pending battle in the Lord's hands, but he still formulated a strategy, gave his brother and the troops a pep talk, marched out to encounter the enemy courageously, and fought hard.

In several places in the New Testament, the apostle Paul compared the Christian life to athletic competition (see 1 Cor. 9:24-27 for one example). The competitive athlete is more aggressive than the weekend sports buff who is merely trying to burn a few calories. Paul's example as someone who *pressed on,* was *reaching forward,* and was going after *the goal for the prize* stirred his readers to be equally sincere about their faith. With his words and life, Paul said, "Do what you can. Give your best effort. God will fill in the distance between your performance and perfection with His grace."

On Mount Moriah, Abraham discovered that God was his provider, but he still did plenty of work himself (see Gen. 12:8-9; 14:14-16; 21:25-26; 22:14). Abraham did not expect God to work miracles for him every day so he would never have to struggle, sweat, suffer, or sob. He trusted God to take care of him, but he still pastured his livestock, set up and took down his tents, built altars, dug wells, and fought battles. Christians who think trusting in God means they can adopt a passive attitude toward life live in denial of the clear teaching of both the Old and New Testaments (see Prov. 24:30-34; 2 Thess. 3:6-10). To trust God for a new job does not mean you sit at home waiting for the phone to ring. Instead, you pray, write your résumé, and then knock on doors. You do what you can. Sure wish he could help with the question: so what's the difference/balance in doing what I can and doing God's work for him, as mentioned previously.

I can gratefully say God has always been faithful to my family and me through the years. When I say God has definitely supplied our needs, I mean sometimes He provided me work outside the ministry to cover our monthly bills. Of course, on other occasions God took care of us in other interesting and miraculous ways—like finding a bag of groceries on our porch when we did not have money for dinner or receiving an unexpected check in the mail when we would not have been able to pay our rent otherwise. But most often, God brought opportunities my way to work extra jobs. In this way, He met our needs.

When we lived in Huntington Beach, we could not stretch my salary far enough to meet simple needs, like tennis shoes for our sons—who seemed either to outgrow or wear out a pair of shoes each month. Fortunately, Smith Brothers' Mortuary was not far from our house, and after performing a couple of funeral services there, they asked if I was interested in making a few extra dollars once in awhile. I assumed they meant conducting services for people who did not have a minister, but after their first call to let me know a body needed to be picked up and brought to the mortuary, I realized what they had in mind. After dropping off my "delivery," they paid me five dollars. The uncanny thing about that job was just about the time we were ready to put cardboard in the soles of our sons' shoes, the phone would ring, and I was told Hoag Hospital needed two bodies to be transferred to the mortuary. Although the calls came in the middle of the night and dragged me out of bed, I would pray, "Thank you, Lord, for meeting our needs."

The wonder of God is that He allows us to participate in His work, He encourages us to do what we do best, He is pleased to see us grow to our fullest potential. So if you think God is going to allow you to lie in bed, open your mouth, and say, "OK, God, if you want me to eat today, drop food into my mouth and I'll chew it," then you do not know the Scripture or the ways of God—not to mention that your mental library is missing a few volumes. God does not work that way. Trusting Him is never an excuse for laziness. He wants us to do what we can, and in this way demonstrate our love and obedience. He will meet us there and take us the rest of the way.

IS IT YOUR BEST?

During the Nixon presidency, former Ambassador Winston Lord was called upon to write speeches for both President Nixon and Henry Kissinger—a task he would not wish on his worst enemies. According to an interview in *The National Security Archives*, Kissinger was not only a speechwriter himself but also a demanding boss. On one famous occasion, Lord entered Kissinger's office with the draft of a speech and set it on his desk.

"He called me in the next day," Lord explains, "and said, 'Is this the best you can do?' I said, 'Henry, I thought so, but I'll try again.' So I go back in a few days and write another draft.

He called me in the next day and he said, 'Are you sure this is the best you can do?' I said, 'Well, I really thought so. I'll try one more time.'

Anyway, this went on eight times with eight drafts; each time he said, 'Is this the best you can do?' So I went in his office with a ninth draft, and when he called me in the next day and asked me that same question, I got exasperated and I said, 'Henry, I've beaten my brains out—this is the ninth draft. I know it's the best I can do: I can't possibly improve one more word.'

He then looked at me and said, 'In that case, now I'll read it.'"

Have you ever heard someone shrug off a poor job by saying, "It's good enough for government work"? Contrast that statement with what Paul said in Colossians 3:23-24, *And whatever you do, do it heartily, as to the Lord and not to men, knowing that from the Lord you will receive the reward of the inheritance; for you serve the Lord Christ.* You will never have to second-guess yourself or your work if you give God your best. Of course, giving him your best does not mean you are perfect. In fact, the best I could do sometimes meant I fell flat on my face or made a mess of my circumstances. Even so, I can sleep well at night because I know I gave God my best effort and I commit the results to Him.

The only time I am troubled is when I know I have not done my best work or gave my whole heart to the project. Then, if problems follow, I realize they are my own fault. But when I know I have put my best thinking and energy into my work, and everything else is up to the Lord, then I have perfect comfort and assurance. If failure follows my best effort, then I have no reason to be eaten up with remorse or anxiety; I am not able to give any more than my best.

Some people are so afraid of failure they do not do anything. Their philosophy seems to be: If I do not do anything, then I will not make any mistakes. But to do nothing is an even bigger mistake. Jesus warned us against hiding our talent in the ground because we are afraid of making a mistake with what we have been given (see Matt. 25:14-30). We need to be investors, putting our talents and skills and gifts to work for the kingdom, giving our best effort, and not concerning ourselves with whether our return is tenfold, twenty-fold, or sixty-fold because the results are up to God.

God does not always appoint the most qualified person to His mission. He is often more interested in availability and ability. The Bible is full of stories of under-qualified men and women who tried to shrink back from the destiny to which God had called them. They said, "I belong to the least significant tribe of Is-rael," "I cannot speak well," and "I am only a child," as they tried to wriggle out of His call on their lives. Have you ever considered the reason you are not qualified to do the work to which God has called you is because you are not qualified for it, and for that rea-son you must rely on Him and cannot help but give Him the credit when it succeeds?

God will always give more than you give, do more than you do, and multiply the results of your labor. If God limited His work to people who were talented, capable, or credentialed, there would be no mystery to His accomplishments and little glory to His account. We would all praise the talented people. But in using *the foolish things of the world to put to shame the wise* and *the weak things of the world to put to shame the things which are mighty; and the base things of the world and the things which are despised . . . and the things which are not, to bring to nothing the things that are, that no flesh should glory in His presence;* God alone receives the credit and the glory *(1 Cor. 1:27-29).*

When I was playing softball with our church teams, we called some players "glory hogs." These were the ones who tried to catch every fly ball or make every out, even if the ball was in another player's zone. Each one of us has the potential of being a glory hog, but God wants us to be fully aware of how much we depend on Him and how much He is actually involved in our lives. So when we give God our best and leave the rest up to Him, we see His greatness compensate for our weakness and take our work further than we could ever hope.

God may be tapping you on the shoulder right now, saying, "I will show you the work I have in mind for you." Then, as you offer all those great excuses why you cannot possibly do the job He wants you to do, with every excuse you are qualifying yourself for His use. Moses, Gideon, King Saul, Isaiah, Jeremiah, and Peter all saw themselves as inadequate, unqualified, and unworthy of God's call, yet He used them all in history-making ways.

God Is Our Strength

Joab and Abishai were caught in a trap, their troops surrounded by the enemy, and they faced the danger of panic gripping their soldiers. The result would be certain defeat and disaster. But after formulating a reasonable strategy, Joab told his brother, *"Be of good courage, and let us be strong for our people and for the cities of our God. And may the Lord do what is good in His sight"(2 Sam. 10:12).*

At some point, almost everyone feels like giving up. You may think, "What's the use in putting up a fight? I'm overwhelmed. All the power, money, and control is in the hands of the opposition." You are ready to surrender to despair, injustice, or evil without even putting up a fight. But with our lives and work committed to God, there is no reason to let our hands fall to our sides because the battle is too big, the enemy too strong, or our own strength too small.

If you are faced with serious difficulty, hardship, and heartache and cannot see a way out, ask yourself if you have done your best. If you answer "yes," but you still need help and direction from God, then commit your way and your circumstances to the Lord. He will give you the strategy and the courage; He will enable you to be valiant in the face of danger and opposition. After you have done your best, you will be amazed at what God does on your behalf.

Against the force of your doubt, summon what courage you have and fight for everything important to you. Then let God do what is good in His sight, because if it is good in His sight, it will be good in your sight too!

Finally, my brethren, be strong in the Lord and in the power of His might (Eph. 6:10).

Prayer

Lord God,
forgive us for sometimes surrendering to temptation
without a fight.
Forgive us for giving in to despair without calling
on You.
Forgive us our inactivity.
We know the truth,
that unless You build the house, we labor in vain;
and we know that You have called us to give our best,
but we do not always have the wisdom to do so.
So today open up Your treasures of grace
and enable us to draw on a potential
we never knew we had.
Then, as we commit everything to You,
show us Your might, wisdom, and glory!
Brand this important truth on our hearts;
for we trust in You, O Lord.
Through Jesus' name.
Amen.

CHAPTER 4

Seeing the Invisible

And Elisha prayed, and said, "Lord, I pray,
open his eyes that he may see." Then the
Lord opened the eyes of the young man, and
he saw. And behold the mountain was full of
horses and chariots of fire all around Elisha.

(2 Kin. 6:17)

THE SETTING

The Syrian king, Ben-Hadad, was furious with his
army officers because, although he was at war with Israel, every time he launched a campaign, the Israelite
troops seemed to have advance warning of his position. On more than one occasion, Israel was able to
evade being ambushed by the Syrians. Ben-Hadad
was convinced one of his trusted advisers was leaking
information to the king of Israel. So he called them
into his war room and said, *"Will you not show me
which of us is for the king of Israel?" (2 Kin. 6:11).*
His officers affirmed their innocence and explained
to him a prophet in Israel knew the words the king
spoke in his bedroom. Elisha was the one responsible
for warning the king of Israel of Syrian positions, *not*

just once or twice (2 Kin. 6:8-10). Elisha's uncanny knowledge of Syrian intelligence is not at all unusual in light of his many insights God gave him regarding distant events. He was surprised only when God did *not* tell him what was happening in other places (see 2 Kin. 4:27). We would probably do well to note the term *prophet* was a late title. Before it was used in Israel, such people were referred to as *seers (1 Sam. 9:9).*

The way this episode is beginning to unfold gives us the feeling Elisha is unlike other characters who appear in the story. Everyone other than Elisha is limited to the ways information is normally communicated between people in the world. Elisha, however, is connected to an information source that lifts his knowledge above the world described in the text. He seems to know as much as the storyteller and the readers. No one else in Israel knew what the Syrians discussed, and the king of Israel had to send reconnaissance missions to confirm Elisha's warnings. So early on, we become aware of Elisha's interaction with the supernatural, although we have no idea how that occurs.

Ben-Hadad sent a large contingent of soldiers to find and capture Elisha. They arrived at the city of Dothan at night and surrounded the city. When Eilsha's servant arose in the morning and saw the Syrians, he cried, *"Alas, my master! What shall we do?"* (2 Kin. 6:15). Before we assume he was a coward, crying, "We're doomed," we should imagine ourselves in his situation. A great army with infantry, horses, and chariots was ready to launch an attack against an unarmed village. The soldiers, who had a reputation for showing merciless cruelty to their defeated enemies, were brandishing their swords and spears. Dothan and its inhabitants had no reason for hope.

But Elisha answered, *"Do not fear, for those who are with us are more than those who are with them"* (2 Kin. 6:16). Then Elisha prayed the request quoted above, *"Lord, I pray, open his eyes that he may see."* With that, his servant took another look, and this time he saw more than the Syrian soldiers; he saw the mountain-side *"full of horses and chariots of fire all around Elisha."* We cannot help but wonder what the young man had to say about *that* spectacle.

But Elisha was not yet finished with his morning prayers. When the Syrians advanced on him, he prayed, *"Strike this people, I pray, with blindness."* This prayer is for the reverse effect he had requested for his servant; one person's eyes were opened and an army's eyes were blinded. The rest of the story would fall under the literary category of comedy, as Elisha nonchalantly approached the blinded soldiers and told them, *"This is not the way, and this is not the city. Follow me, and I will bring you to the man you seek."* He then led them inside the walled city of Samaria, where they were surrounded by Israel's warriors. *Then Elisha prayed, "Lord, open the eyes of these men, that they may see,"* and what they saw was terrifying.

The king of Israel was beside himself, and franti-cally cried to Elisha, *"My father, shall I kill them? Shall I kill them?"* Fortunately, Elisha didn't seek revenge, but answered the king in a humane and generous way, *"Would you kill those whom you have taken captive with your sword and your bow?"* He then told the king to

give the Syrians food and water and release them
(2 Kin. 6:17-23).

The prophets refused to accept the conventional
viewpoint, the reality everyone else accepted, the majority opinion. They believed there was always more
to a situation than what meets the eye. So they
strained to see what might be present, but invisible to
others with limited imagination and faith.

OPEN HIS EYES

What a wonderful gift Elisha shared with his servant
when he asked God to open his eyes. A story is found
earlier in the Old Testament where the pagan prophet
Balaam was hired by the king of Moab to curse Israel
as they traveled through their territory. God's angel
stood on the road to stand against Balaam, and kill
him if necessary. Balaam did not see the angel, but his
donkey saw him, and three times protected Balaam
from being skewered. Only after the hot-tempered
prophet beat his donkey did the angel open his eyes
so he could see him (see Num. 22:1-35). Later, in his
prophetic blessing, Balaam referred to himself as the
man *who hears the words of God, Who sees the vision of
the Almighty, Who falls down, with eyes wide open*
(Num. 24:4, 15-16). Can you imagine if we walked
through our natural world with *eyes wide open* to a
larger reality?

When Jesus asked two blind beggars why they were
screaming, *"Have mercy on us,"* and what it was they
wanted Jesus to do for them, they told Jesus, *"Lord,
that our eyes may be opened"* (Matt. 20:29-34). Jesus had

the power to open, not only the eyes of the blind to physical sight, but the eyes of His disciples to spiritual sight. When He first approached two disciples walking to Emmaus after His resurrection, *"their eyes were prevented from recognizing Him" (Luke 24:13-16, NASB).* When they saw Jesus bless and break bread with them at dinner, *Then their eyes were opened and they knew Him,* and, ironically, *He vanished from their sight (Luke 24:30-31).* Later, when Jesus appeared to His eleven apostles, *He opened their understanding, that they might comprehend the Scriptures (Luke 24:45).*

Very few people in the history of the world have been blessed to have their eyes opened in this supernatural way and to see as clearly into this other reality as Elisha and his servant. Even the other seers, prophets, and apostles did not see as definitely or precisely as Elisha. The only other biblical character who comes close is Jesus, who saw not only what His Heavenly Father was doing but also knew the thoughts of others. If God did not intend to open our eyes in the same way, why is this story in the Bible? Why are we tantalized with this fascinating awareness and foreknowledge only to have it withdrawn from us?

I do not know for certain whether God intends for other gifted believers to be able to see as Elisha did or even to the degree of Paul and other New Testament prophets. The benefit I derive from these stories is simply knowing the other reality is out there, that I am not alone, and no matter what my circumstances, "Those who are with me are more than those who are against me."

HOW CAN THIS BE?

Physicists are aware of three fundamental forces in the universe: gravity, the electroweak force, and the color force (or strong force). What physicists have not yet determined is how gravity is joined to the other two forces. During the 1980s, the "string theory" was proposed to solve the problem, but it lost steam until new research revived it in the 1990s. If string theory actually explains the three forces, then physics will place at our fingertips a theory of everything.

One quirk of string theory is that to accommodate it, our universe must be comprised of 11 dimensions rather than the four dimensions of space-time as we know them by sense experience. Our four-dimensional universe is sometimes referred to as braneworld—as in mem*brane*—which can be compared to the dry surface of gravy when it has been sitting in a bowl in the open air. The particles of our four-dimensional experience cannot escape this braneworld that we inhabit. But other particles move through the brane and bulk dimensions.

Naturally there is a great deal of speculation—and genuine research—among theoretical physicists and fringe mystics regarding the possibility of other universes that exist alongside or even penetrate our universe. A different set of laws of physics apply in these places. If this is so, then we are obviously oblivious to these parallel realities, even though they actually exist. Beings in another universe who knew how to communicate by way of particles that move freely through dimensions—gravitons, perhaps—could arguably communicate with intelligent minds in other universes.

When we look at a biblical worldview, we see a universe penetrated by messages and beings who belong to another reality, yet know how to appear and communicate—and even interact—with living organisms in our reality. Interestingly, the Hebrew word for *angel* is the same word for a *messenger*. The New Testament explains that angels are *ministering spirits sent forth to minister for those who will inherit salvation (Heb. 1:14).* Invisible to our eyes, intelligent and powerful agents are nearby to assist us through our spiritual journey with God (see Ps. 91:11-12).

What are we supposed to do with this information? How does it help us to have this knowledge of angels as ministers sent from God? There are several spiritual benefits, but what I wish to point out here is the mere fact of *those who are with us* can help us become more conscious of God and His divine resources. Paul explained that Christians do *not look at the things which are seen, but the things which are not seen. For the things which are seen are temporary, but the things which are not seen are eternal (2 Cor. 4:18).* When our minds get stuck in our material world and temporary circumstances, we panic and say, "Alas, my master! What shall we do?" But we can immediately dissolve that panic simply by shifting our concentration from the immediate and physical to the eternal and spiritual.

In *The Great Divorce*, C. S. Lewis provides the reader with a wonderful description of heaven, which, even though fictional, creates the feeling it will certainly be no less than what he pictures for us. First he noticed he was in a "larger space" than he experienced on earth, "as if the sky were further off and the extent of the green plain wider than they could be on this little ball of earth." He felt as if he had somehow emerged from worldly reality into a space that made the solar system seem as if it existed indoors. Next he noticed the objects in heaven seemed "so much solider than things in our country that men were ghosts by comparison." Thinking of heaven as a "solider" dimension than the one we now inhabit, a reality that makes ours seem like its shadow by comparison, is a lovely image that helps us loosen our grip on the things of this earth and wonder what it would be like to truly *seek first the kingdom of God (Matt. 6:33).*

FIGHTING THE INVISIBLE MAN

You are no doubt familiar with Paul's famous analogy in Ephesians where he explained, *we do not wrestle against flesh and blood, but against principalities, against powers, against the rulers of the darkness of this age, against spiritual hosts of wickedness in the heavenly places (Eph. 6:12).* Imagine that! We are engaged in a struggle with an enemy we cannot see. In H. G. Wells' *The Invisible Man*, the victims of the deranged scientist found it impossible to defeat him because they could not protect themselves from his invisible blows nor return any punches to the body they could not see. If we are in a conflict with spiritual forces, then we need to be reminded constantly to suit up with the only protection against their invisible attack: the *whole armor of God (Eph. 6:13-18)*.

Fortunately we have weapons that, like this warfare, are not flesh and blood, but *mighty in God for pulling down strongholds, casting down arguments and every high thing that exalts itself against the knowledge of God, bringing every thought into captivity to the obedience of Christ (2 Cor. 10:4-5).* So if an invisible attack of doubt is launched against our minds, or despair against our emotions, illness against our bodies, irritation and frustration against our relationships with others, or rebellion against God, we can fight back. Being unaware of the source of these assaults puts us at a serious disadvantage. But if we *are not ignorant of his devices*, then we can prevent Satan from taking *advantage of us (2 Cor. 2:11)*.

Elisha's servant panicked until *the Lord opened his eyes*, and then he saw they were in no danger whatsoever; rather, the Syrians were in trouble. What we are able to see with our eyes is merely the physical manifestation of a situation that is spiritual at its roots. We look at and try to resolve mere symptoms when we need to address the real problem. On the surface, we see no more than what the young man could see, and like him, we panic. "Alas, I'm surrounded! There's no hope. I don't have enough money. My troubles are too many. I've run out of ideas. I'm going down for sure." But a simple turn of attention toward heaven, and that fear evaporates into thin air.

Listen to the prayer of Jehoshaphat, king of Judah, when he was in a similar situation, *"O our God, will You not judge them? For we have no power against this great multitude that is coming against us; nor do we know what to do, but our eyes are upon You"* (2 Chr. 20:12). Do you see how his circumstances looked from a natural viewpoint? He did not have enough strength, the opposition had too much strength, and he did not know what to do. So what could he do? Look away from himself and his circumstances to God. What was God's response? *"Do not be afraid nor dismayed because of this great multitude, for the battle is not yours, but God's"* (2 Chr. 20:15).

If we are not able to shift to a spiritual perspective, then we are vulnerable to despair and the hopelessness that plagues our world. The horses and chariots of fire let us know that, regardless of the formidable dangers in our circumstances, God has everything under control and He is working out everything for our good. If we cannot see the horses and chariots with our own eyes, then we have God's promise to bring us through to victory. Every "danger, toil and snare" looks so wonderfully different when our spiritual eyes are opened.

BLIND FAITH

Is it blind faith to hope in God when the world crumbles all around us, to believe God will walk us through heartache and loss? Is it blind faith to rest in the assurance that nothing can separate us from the love of God, not even death? No, it is not blind faith if our eyes have been opened. We cannot say that faith is blind if with it we see more, not less, than others see with only their natural vision. The person who truly believes sees more than the person who cannot see past the shadow world of this life into the "solider" kingdom of God.

Imagine someone pointing to a bead of water on a leaf and saying, "There is death in that droplet." You respond, "I don't see any danger in it. Why do you say it's deadly?" Then the other person says, "Let me show you," and puts the waterdrop on a slide and under a microscope. You look at the drop magnified and see logs of squirming creatures not visible to the naked eye. "Do you see those amoebas? They're deadly."

Both dangers and resources are invisible to natural sight; good and evil, help and harm, angels of fire and fiery arrows are present. With our eyes open, we will not take a beating from our invisible enemy nor will we miss out on the peace, power, and victory of God's divine support. Most importantly, we have a strategy we can use daily as we suit up in the armor of God: to be *praying always with all prayer and supplication in the Spirit (Eph. 6:18).* We pray *in the Spirit* because that is the arena of our fiercest struggles. For our modern uniform we might include the goggles of hope to go into each day with our eyes opened.

If you had the gift of spiritual perception, you could draw your attention away from troubling issues that are only physical and transient. If you could look upon the things unseen and eternal, then you would be lifted out of hopelessness and despair into the triumph and victory of Jesus our Lord (see Col. 2:11-15; 3:1-4).

As Elisha prayed for his servant, so I pray for you and me, "O God, open our eyes."

Prayer

Father,
thank You for the marvelous victory we enjoy
in Jesus Christ our Lord.
You have filled our hearts with joyous relief
and our mouths with praise,
for we are no longer defeated by life,
but we walk in the power of Your Spirit.
Our afflictions are light and but for a moment,
but You are working through them a weight of glory
that far exceeds them and is eternal.
So we pray that You would open our eyes;
give us fresh spiritual insight,
let us see that You are for us
and nothing can be against us.
In Jesus' name.
Amen.

Chapter 5

He Sees, He Hears, He Knows

And the Lord said: "I have surely seen the oppression of My people who are in Egypt, and have heard their cry because of their taskmasters, for I know their sorrows. So I have come down to deliver them out of the hand of the Egyptians, and to bring them to a good and large land, to a land flowing with milk and honey, to the place of the Canaanites and the Hittites and the Amorites and the Perizzites and the Hivites and the Jebusites."

(Ex. 3:7-8)

To See or Not to See

According to Stephen, the heroic martyr in the Book of Acts, the life of Moses consisted of three spans of 40 years. For the first 40 years, Moses grew up in the house of Pharaoh where he was educated *in all the wisdom of the Egyptians (Acts 7:22-23)*. For the next 40 years, he became a shepherd and *dweller in the land of*

Midian (Acts 7:29-30). During the last 40 years of his life, Moses lived in the wilderness as a shepherd to the people of Israel (see Acts 7:35-36). I once heard someone cleverly observe Moses spent 40 years thinking he was a somebody, another 40 learning he was a nobody, and another 40 discovering God can take a nobody and make him a somebody.

Moses began the second stage of his life when one day he noticed a small fire on one of the ascents of Mount Sinai. After observing the flames for awhile, he realized the fire was neither spreading nor dying out, and the bush in flames did not burn up. He decided to climb the mountainside for a closer investigation, but as he approached the phenomenon, God's voice spoke to him from the flame and commanded him to remove his sandals, for the place where he stood was *holy ground (Ex. 3:5).* Afraid, Moses hid his face as God explained why He had *come down,* and that brings us to the verse quoted above.

And the Lord said, "I have surely seen the oppression of My people," (Ex. 3:7-8). A close reading beginning in Exodus 2 reveals that *vision* is an important subtheme. In fact, the verbs *see, saw, seeing,* and *seen* shape the structure of the plot in the beginning of this story. Let me illustrate what I mean. When Moses' mother *saw* that he was beautiful, she spared his life (Ex. 2:2). Later, Pharaoh's daughter *saw* Moses' basket-boat floating in the Nile (Ex. 2:5). When she removed the lid, she *saw* the child (Ex. 2:6). After he had grown to adulthood, Moses went out and *looked* at the burdens of the Israelites and *saw* an Egyptian beating a Hebrew (Ex. 2:11). He then *looked* this way and that to make sure no one else was watching, and killed the Egyptian (Ex. 2:12). The last word of chapter two is that God *looked upon the children of Israel and God, and acknowledged them (Ex. 2:23-25).*

We are not quite finished with this biblical exercise. In Exodus 3, Moses *saw* the burning bush and decided to *see* why it was not consumed. When God saw that Moses turned aside to *look*, He stopped him (Ex. 3:2-4). God then told Moses that He had *seen* the oppression of His people (Ex. 3:7, 9). In all cases, the italicized words in this paragraph and the one above translate the same Hebrew. Further down we will come back to this thread and find an additional feature that adds spiritual substance to the story. But for now we will meditate on the fact that the Lord is the *God-Who-Sees (Gen. 16:13).*

In Psalm 139, David gives a beautiful, poetic description of God's complete knowledge of him. Using the same Hebrew word *to see,* he says, *Your eyes saw my substance, being yet unformed (v. 16).* He also invites God to search him *and see if there is any wicked way in me (v. 24).* His poem leaves us uncertain whether David finds God's constant observation comforting or frightening. On the one hand, there is nowhere he can get away from God's presence (or *face*), as if there were divine security cameras everywhere (vv. 7-12). But on the other hand, David praises God for His intimate knowledge of his formation in utero and the multitude of God's thoughts toward him (vv. 13-18). Perhaps knowing God never takes His eyes from us always has this binary effect—frightening and comforting at the same time.

In another poem, David reflects on the wicked who think God does not see their thefts and murders. But David challenges them, saying, *He who planted the ear, shall He not hear? He who formed the eye, shall He not see? (Ps. 94:9).* Sometimes my circumstances are difficult and distressing. Knowing God sees what I am suffering is a great relief. Other times, if I know my actions contradict God's will, then knowing He sees me is terrifying. So I suppose the heart of the matter depends on me, whether I find God's ever-present gaze reassuring or discomforting.

Imagine for a moment you have a choice between God's eyes burning a hole through you (see Ps. 11:4-6) or keeping you as the *apple of His eye (Ps. 17:8).* He is not looking for sin and evil, but to the contrary, His eyes scour the earth looking for human hearts loyal to Him (see 2 Chr. 16:9). His eyes *run to and fro throughout the whole earth* to find people who are seeking Him (Ps. 14:2). We cannot hold God responsible for what He sees us doing, but we can expect Him to respond to what we are doing in a manner appropriate to our actions (see Ps. 18:25-27). However, the wonderful truth is that at all times we can rest that we live before God's compassionate and sympathetic eyes.

If there is encouragement in the Old Testament promise that God sees His people at all times and in every situation, Jesus Christ emphasized blessing and benefit of God's careful observation even more. God sees every gift given, every prayer made, and every missed meal *in secret* and openly rewards His faithful followers (see Matt. 6:1-18). He knows what we need before we even ask (see Matt. 6:8, 32). God is not unaware of the sparrow, nearly worthless to humans, so how much more attention will He pay to humans who are *of more value than many sparrows*? In fact, He is conscious of the most minute issues of our lives, including how many hairs are on our heads (see Luke 12:7).

You do not need to worry God will ever lose track of you. Even people who have tried to hide from God found it impossible. Adam and Eve headed for the trees and Jonah headed for the seas, but they did not get very far. We already saw that Moses *looked this way and that*, then killed the Egyptian, thinking no one could see him. But the mistake in looking over both shoulders is that you forget to look up to know One who always sees everything. You will never turn invisible to God; He loves you too much to take His eyes off you, and He paid too great a price for you ever to risk losing His investment.

God saw the misery of His people, that they were in great distress and treated cruelly. He assured Moses, *"I have surely seen the oppression of My people who are in Egypt"* (Ex. 3:7).

DOES GOD "BUG" US?

God was not only moved by the sight of Israel in Egypt, but He also *heard their cry (Ex. 3:7)*. Human slavery is among the worst institutions of social cruelty this world has ever known. The inhumanity of slave owners from all times and in all places is one of the greatest marks against humankind. Seeing that all people are created in God's image should be sufficient reason to deter a believer from treating another person as

a possession. If passages in the Bible seem to treat slavery neutrally, the devoted follower of Jesus Christ will
refuse to subjugate others to their service or control because Jesus turned heathen hierarchies upside down.
The great ones of His kingdom make themselves servants to others, while rejecting a place where they
would lord their authority over others (see Matt. 20:25-
27). Perhaps Paul's highest moral comment on this
subject is that in Christ all believers are equal; the spiritual community does not recognize ethnic, class, or
gender differences (see Gal. 3:26-28). All believers are
on the same level when they stand before the Lord.

Have you ever felt God did not hear your cry of distress? We would be surprised, I think, to find a person
who had never had this feeling, for whom it seemed
their prayers hit the ceiling and fell back unheard and
unanswered. The poets who poured out their hearts
in the psalms certainly knew what it was to feel that
God had turned a deaf ear to them. They frequently
began their prayers with the request that God would
hear them (see Ps. 4:1; 5:1; 64:1; etc.). What does this
mean when it seems our prayers die on our lips or return to us like undeliverable mail?

No matter what our hearts feel or our doubts tell us,
a prayer is not spoken that God does not hear. In fact,
His willingness to hear prayer is the reason all people
will come to Him (see Ps. 65:2). Sometimes we make
reference to God in language that specifically applies
to humans to make sense out of His divine nature and
dealings with human. Unfortunately, using our limited vocabulary has the liability of damaging our the-
ology. The truth is, a word is not spoken, but that God

knows it thoroughly (see Ps. 139:4). God is eaves-dropping; He has your phone tapped and your house bugged. As we saw in an earlier chapter, you cannot speak a word in your bedroom with the door closed that God does not hear.

When you cry, God hears you. We can say even more because David prayed, *Give heed to the voice of my cry, My King and my God (Ps. 5:2).* Every parent knows their child's cry is like a voice. Sometimes a child cries merely for attention; other times he cries in frustration. I have seen a lot of fake crying in my years of parenting and grandparenting. But there is a cry of pain and anguish that a parent cannot ignore. God hears the voice of your cry.

Have you ever found yourself absolutely amazed the Creator of the universe will listen to what you have to say, will regard your request, and will many times give you the very thing you ask—and sometimes give you something even better? Tommy Walker has written a song titled "He Knows My Name" in which we worship God, singing, "He sees each tear that falls, and He hears me when I call." Yes! Amazing as it is, God hears *me* when I call.

In my own experience, tears have a power to reach a human heart. Even walking through a mall, if I see a stranger sitting on a bench or by a fountain crying, I feel compelled to ask if I can be of help. Something about tears draws sympathy from other human hearts. Your tears affect God, your Father, in the same way. He sees, He hears, He knows our sorrows.

God also told Moses, *"I know their sorrows"* (or *pain*). Few people understand the sorrow and grief of another (see Prov. 14:10). To fully appreciate the soul-deep agony of grief, you must walk through it for yourself. The gut-wrenching pain of loss cannot be learned from a textbook or lecture. So people who say, "I understand" to a mother who is suffering over the death of her child do her a disservice if they have not passed through that dark valley. Pain speaks to pain—or in the words of the poet, *Deep calls unto deep at the noise of Your waterfalls (Ps. 42:7),* which is the same psalm that says, *O my God, my soul is cast down within me (v. 6),* which is a beautiful way of describing depression.

Should we be surprised Isaiah the prophet described Jesus the Messiah as *A Man of sorrows and acquainted with grief? (Is. 53:3).* When Jesus says, "I understand," and you look into His eyes, you know He is speaking the truth. He knows suffering and grief. His soul was *exceedingly sorrowful, even to death (Mark 14:34).* He knew that suffocating sadness that makes your chest feel like it will cave in.

This God who sees your broken heart and hears the cry of your voice, knows all about the distress in your life, the anxieties that tear at your soul, the weariness that hangs on your limbs. He knows your fear, doubt, temptation, longing, ambition, despair, hope, love, and everything else that can be known about you.

GOD, THE DOER OF HIS WORD

God saw the oppression and heard the groaning of Israel, but that was not the extent of His concern. He went one more, very important step with Moses. God told Moses, *"I have come down to deliver them" (Ex. 3:8).*

How wonderful it is that God sees our tears, hears our cry, and knows our sorrow. But if He went no further, we would not benefit much, even if He were infinitely sympathetic. Imagine if God's love operated the way ours tends to operate toward each other. We are too much like the hypothetical believer James described when he said, *"If a brother or sister is naked and destitute of daily food, and one of you says to them, 'Depart in peace, be warmed and filled,' but you do not give them the things which are needed for the body, what does it profit?'"*

"O God, do You know what's going on?"

"Yes, My child, I see."

"O God, I need Your help."

"Yes, child, I hear you."

"Lord, my body is racked with pain and my mind is darkened with despair!"

"Yes, I know all there is to know about your mind, body, and situation."

If God went no further than mere words of reassurance, then *what does it profit?* But God said, *"I have seen . . . I have heard, . . . and I have come down to deliver."*

I said earlier we would return to the thread of "seeing" that runs through these chapters, and now is the time to re-examine this theme. Carefully re-read Exodus 2 and 3, then ask: What happens after someone *sees* a specific scene? What happens after Moses' mother *sees* that he is a beautiful child, Pharaoh's daughter *sees* the basket, Moses *sees* the Egyptian, and so on? You will notice in each case that "sight" is followed by *action*. So when we come to God's message to Moses, that He had *seen* the oppression of His people, He also came down prepared to take action. The story has prepared us to expect a significant turn of events, because so far only humans have seen another person here or there and their actions have been somewhat limited. However, God has seen a whole nation oppressed by another nation, and He has no limit in His ability to take action.

God said, *"I have seen, . . ."* and by now we have caught the rhythm of this theme, so we know the ball is in God's court. In light of this revelation, consider the story Matthew reported when Jesus tried to leave for a deserted place to rest with His disciples and they were followed by a large crowd. *And Jesus, when He came out, saw a great multitude and was moved with compassion for them, because they were like sheep not having a shepherd. So He began to teach them many things (Mark 6:34).* Jesus saw the people, was moved with compassion, and taught them. A little while later, He fed them as well (see Mark 6:41-42).

Jesus, the Man of sorrows, *sees* your distress, He *hears* your cry, and to His loving eyes, you look like a stray sheep. So He comes down to where you live to teach, feed, and heal you. No, we cannot see Him as we would like—we are still waiting for Him to open our eyes. But we can love and trust Him. . . . *whom having not seen you love. Though now you do not see Him, yet believing, you rejoice with joy inexpressible and full of glory, receiving the end of your faith—the salvation of your souls (1 Pet. 1:8-9).* When you pray, know this: Jesus sees you; He sees you stretching your faith toward Him, seeking Him, longing for Him with all your heart and soul. Jesus seeing you is far more important than being able to see Him.

THE COST OF CARING

What does it cost to care for someone else? The day Jesus rode a donkey into Jerusalem, the people cried, "Save now." Their request was explicit in what they wanted Jesus to do for them, and when they wanted Him to do it. They wanted Him to save them, and they wanted to see the fulfillment of their apocalyptic longing that very day.

Somewhere on the Mount of Olives, Jesus *saw the city and wept over it (Luke 19:41).* He wept because His deepest desire was to "save" them; to "deliver" them as God had delivered Israel from Egypt so many centuries earlier. But what the people clamoring for salvation did not realize was the nature of the salvation Jesus offered and what it would cost Him to provide it. They shouted joyfully, imagining their exile had almost come to an end and God was about to return to Zion. They could imagine themselves free from the Romans, the Persians, the Egyptians, and other nations that threatened their existence.

Jesus wept because they were blind to the true chains that bound them to slavery. Even His disciples did not understand to be delivered from sin and guilt was the great liberation. Sin had enslaved the world, and from heaven God said, "I see the darkness spread across the earth, wrapping itself around the hearts of men, women, and children. I hear the cry of victims who have suffered the violence of evil and the oppression of temptation. I know their sorrow and have come down to deliver them."

You know what grieves and pains you. You know

exactly what you need. But do you realize God sees your imprisoned heart and hears its groans as it tries to go on in life under the burden of sin and guilt, shame and confusion? God sent His Son to deliver you from the power of evil, to give birth to a new and wonderful life within you, and to release you into the *glorious liberty of the children of God (Rom. 8:21).* A life of joy, blessing, and freedom awaits you, if you are willing to accept God's deliverance.

Prayer

Heavenly Father,
we thank You for always seeing,
always listening, always knowing.
You have come down,
in the Person of Your Son, our Lord Jesus Christ,
to reveal Your power and love,
Your majesty and goodness,
Your holiness and compassion.
"Save now," we pray,
but not like the Palm Sunday crowd outside Jerusalem.
Rather, we pray as Your children,
who understand that the greatest gift
is the forgiveness of our sins, the removal of
our chains,
the glorious liberty of the children of God.
Thank You for this new, rich, and wonderful life
in Christ.
For all who read these words
and find that their soul is crying out in pain,

or they are locked up in the powers of darkness,
or their lives are breaking apart,
and they are in despair because there seems to be no
way out;
come down, once again, to their rescue,
and lift them up into the arms of Jesus,
in whose matchless name we pray.
Amen.

CHAPTER 6

Healing Broken Hearts

But the wicked are like the troubled sea,
When it cannot rest,
Whose waters cast up mire and dirt.
"There is no peace,"
Says my God, "for the wicked."

(Is. 57:20-21)

"YOU ARE HERE"

Dropping into a biblical text halfway through a thought is always risky. Biblical interpretation is a challenge even after a lifetime of study. So when approaching a Bible verse that begins with the word *but*, it's a good idea to back up a few verses and examine the previous thought. As we learned in English classes, the word *but* is a disassociated conjunction used to connect two thoughts. So the question we need to answer before jumping into Isaiah 57:20-21 is, "What was the first thought to which this thought is linked?"

From chapter 40, the prophetic word Isaiah spoke is a challenge to and a condemnation of idolatry and its false gods. The flip side of that message is God's promise of comfort, salvation, and restoration to the true Israel—the *remnant*. Isaiah 57 begins with a graphic description of the idolatry adopted by the shepherds of Israel and a warning of a coming disaster that will prove their collection of idols to be completely worthless. But God would also call out spiritual reformers to prepare the way for believers returning to the Lord (Is. 57:14). Once restored, God Himself would make His home *with the contrite and lowly of spirit (Is. 57:15).* In light of this gracious restoration, God proclaimed:

> "I create the fruit of the lips:
> Peace, peace to him that is far off, and to
>   him that is near,"
> Says the Lord; "And I will heal him."
> (Is. 57:19)

So far, so good. We have a general idea of Isaiah's message in this section of the book of his prophecies. But we need to consider more important themes before we move forward. In chapter 48, God explained to His people they could have enjoyed *peace like a river* had they been faithful to Him (Is. 48:18). In language reminiscent of Israel's escape from Egypt, God announced a *second exodus*, this time from Babylon (Is. 48:20). As in the first exodus when God supplied Israel's every need (Deut. 8:1-16), He would be their traveling companion across the burning desert and back into their homeland. God ended His message in chapter 48 with the same statement as in chapter 47, *There is no peace for the wicked (Is. 48:22).*

The prophetic material that leads up to Isaiah 57:20-21 contains a divine offer of *shalom*, of peace. But this offer put Israel in a precarious position with God. If they refused the gift God extended to them, they would find their circumstances and inner life *like the troubled sea which cannot rest*. If they accepted His offer, He would grant them amnesty and forgiveness. God would even go so far as to heal them from their tendency to backslide. They had everything to gain by running to God and everything to lose by resisting Him.

PEACE

Few people in 21st century America have any idea of what God's *perfect peace* is all about. Even though we are the wealthiest people in world history, we are the most anxious and uptight. We live on a moving sidewalk, traveling 65 miles an hour, rushing through life without having an opportunity to stay in one experience long enough to enjoy it. We spend our neurotic lives in houses of cards where worries multiply, which increases our health problems, causes emotional imbalance, weakens our spirits, corrupts our morals, produces more crime, compounds societal dangers, and so on. We think this hamster wheel existence is normal, and if we can get our wheel spinning faster than anyone else, we win. But all we do is build up speed until we crash, wear out, drive everyone else away, lose touch with what is important, or come to a screeching stop only at the grave. One day we have grown old and find ourselves wondering how we let

all the beauty, goodness, and joy of life slip through
our fingers. But if we try to recall those moments, they
are like blurred photographs taken from a moving car.

God's peace is a healing and life-giving river. If we
drink from it, our bodies are refreshed, our health restored, our spirits revived, and our minds renewed.
How sad that few Christians stroll down to the river
each day to dip their feet into the cool water of God's
perfect peace. Why did we reject the *waters of Shiloah
that flow softly (Is. 8:6)?* Why did we forfeit the *peace of
God, which surpasses all understanding (Phil. 4:7)?* In
other words, if *shalom* is the gift of Christ Jesus to His
followers (see John 14:27), then why are we so tense,
angry, fearful, and upset? We have lost our way to the
river, and the arid, frenetic atmosphere of our everyday lives is killing our souls with thirst.

Consider the many ways God has attempted to either place His peace within us or bring us into His
peace. For example, He gave the priests authority to
place His name on the children of Israel through the
famous benediction in Numbers 6:24-26:

> The Lord bless you and keep you;
> The Lord make His face shine upon you,
> And be gracious to you;
> The Lord lift up His countenance upon you,
> And give you peace.

Later, in the days of the kings of Judah, the Lord
spoke through Isaiah with a promise to the nation of a
coming *Prince of Peace* during whose reign there
would be *no end* to peace (see Is. 9:6-7). On a more per-

sonal level, God promised *perfect peace*—literally, *shalom, shalom* where the repetition intensifies the force of the word—to the person who trusted God and whose mind God supported (see Is. 26:3). Even after Israel returned from their exile in Babylon and Persia, God was still promising peace to His people, *"The glory of this latter temple shall be greater than the former,"* says the Lord of hosts. "And in this place I will give peace," says the Lord of hosts (Hag. 2:9).

When the angels announced Jesus' birth, they said: *"Glory to God in the highest, And on earth peace, goodwill toward men"* (Luke 2:14).

Jesus did not promise His disciples an easy life or one free of conflict. In fact He warned them they would be hated and persecuted. Nevertheless, He reassured them with a guarantee of peace, *"These things I have spoken to you, that in Me you may have peace. In the world you will have tribulation; but be of good cheer, I have overcome the world"* (John 16:33). The world of our daily experience generates tension, temptation, anxiety, and fear, but Jesus has *overcome* that world, so it is possible to live in it without being destroyed by it (see John 17:9-21).

After Jesus returned to His rightful place with God the Father, the apostle Paul began to explore the theological nature of God's peace. He realized people who were at one time *enemies of God* have been *reconciled to God through the death of His Son (Rom. 5:10).* We have laid down our weapons of rebellion against God, and He has set aside the cup of His wrath because Jesus drank from it in our place. Peace *with* God is the foundation of all other experiences and applications of peace. We are no longer at war within ourselves, with others, or with our circumstances. Peace with God leads us into the peace *of* God; that is, a supernatural tranquility that comes to rest in our hearts and is sustained by His Spirit regardless of our circumstances.

Would you like to know how to *experience* God's perfect peace? If you believe Paul's teaching in Romans 5 is a reality in your life, then you are ready to begin enjoying God's peace. But before I tell you the secret, we need to give up a number of cherished myths.

Myth One: To enjoy God's peace, we need to learn all the Bible has to say about it. If it is true God's peace *surpasses* understanding, then we cannot expect to receive it through the narrow opening of our intelligence. You will have to trust God, believe He is smarter than you, and know you can be at peace even though you do not understand His peace or have all the answers to life's riddles and problems.

Myth Two: To enjoy God's peace, we need to apply ourselves to an inflexible and strenuous program of spiritual disciplines. Some people become more anxious and fearful after reading their Bibles; their prayers are more like neurotic chants than communion with God. We do not discover peace in our overactive lives by adding another activity. Peace is more about what we lay down than what we pick up. When God gives you permission to lay down worries, attachments to material possessions, fear, and resentment, His peace floods into the vacancies created by the removal of those negative emotions.

Myth Three: To enjoy God's peace, we have to live sin-less lives. If living a perfectly sinless life is the only way to receive *anything* from God, then we are all in a hopeless state. Yet many believers assume they have no right to expect God to give them the wonderful gift of His peace, because they are mindful of a recent sin they have committed. In many of Paul's New Testament letters, peace immediately follows grace. Grace is God's first invasion of undeserved blessing, and it opens the door for every other blessing—none of which are deserved. In fact, simply believing in the full magnitude of God's grace can flood a person's heart with peace.

Myth Four: To enjoy God's peace, I must do some-thing. Everything that has to be done has been done, so Paul could say Jesus Christ has *made peace through the blood of the cross (Col. 1:20).* Please believe this: You can add nothing to Jesus' work on the cross. The peace that comes from God is a *fruit of the Spirit (Gal. 5:22),* which grows of its own when God's life is teeming within us.

GOD IS NOT A WORRIER

Do you suppose God paces in front of His heavenly throne, wringing His hands while fretting over the outcome of our circumstances? If God does not worry, it is not because He does not care. The Bible is clear on this matter. You are to throw *all your care upon Him, for He cares for you (1 Pet. 5:7).* God is not worried because He knows His purpose for your life. He knows His own power to rescue you, and He knows if you have to travel through suffering or the shadowed valley of death; He is with you to support, guide, and comfort. God also knows that if you should require peace, it will be available to you instantly.

Do I know how to solve all my problems? Ha! Most of the time I do not have the foggiest idea how God plans to get me through my difficulties in one piece. Thankfully, knowing all the answers is not a requisite for basking in God's peace. Oh, sometimes your mind will not let you rest. Here is the conversation that frequently goes on in my head:

"How are you going to get yourself out of this one, Smith?"

"I don't know. I have to leave it with God, and I'm going to trust Him to work it out."

"But how is God going to do *that*?"

"I don't know. But I am at peace with Him regarding this issue."

"What if God doesn't come through in time? What if God wants to drag you through another painful episode in your life?"

Watch out for those "What if?" questions! You will certainly lose God's peace if you start listening to those phobic questions.

My response is, "I don't know, I don't know," and "I don't know!" I do not *need* to know or else God would tell me. All I need to do is *trust*; that is my role in our relationship. God's role is to know; my role is to trust. I find when I trust Him, I am at peace. But having knowledge never gave me peace about anything, and more often than not, it intensified my worries. So you can give it a rest! If God is worried, then I'll worry. If He is at peace, then I can be at peace. He's the pilot, and I'm the passenger. I trust His knowledge and skill.

Peace reproduces itself and extends its effects to others. Unfortunately, anxiety reproduces itself as well. Conflict breeds conflict, hatred breeds hatred, and war breeds war. Has going to war ever put an end to war? Has the human race seen "the war to end all wars"? War is not the end of the sinful and hateful attitudes that push people into war. War merely gives one nation temporary dominance over another, while the hostilities continue to seethe under the surface. The same is true of tension and anxiety; if given reign, they spread tension and anxiety. But they cannot be resolved with more of the same, nor can they switch themselves off. So if I am in constant turmoil, agitation, and unrest, then I will reproduce those feelings in my environment and infect those around me. And that will be the end of our peaceful relations. We will become stiff, contentious, and irritable. But when I know that a beautiful inner peace of God is within me, then I become a peacemaker, a true child of God (see Matt. 5:9). People who angrily scream for peace lose their audience as well as their credibility. But the true peacemaker is at peace with God, himself, and then others.

"I'VE BEEN ROBBED!"

Believers who put their hope and trust in God can know and spread His perfect peace. *But the wicked are like the troubled sea . . . There is no peace for the wicked (Is. 48:22).* We watch our televisions in amazement when a hurricane hits the East and Gulf coasts of the United States. The violence of the winds sends waves crashing over sea walls, flooding streets, and ripping through buildings. The ocean itself is a cauldron of waves, sand, and debris. The tempestuous scenes that flash across our screens are what some people have to live with inside their heads and hearts every day. Jude described them as *raging waves of the sea, foaming up their own shame (Jude 13).* The wicked are not only deprived of peace, but they have to live with an inner gale-force turmoil all the time.

A number of sins are guaranteed to rob a person of God's peace. Any sort of sin attached to desire will never allow a human to rest. These include sexual desire, greed, gluttony, and hunger for power. Caught in those desires, people are deprived of satiation and live instead in a constant state of agitation because they cannot fill their bellies with the *hot east wind,* which is all you get if you *drink iniquity like water (Job 15:2, 16).* Ecclesiastes 5:10 is certainly correct in saying, *He who loves silver will not be satisfied with silver; Nor he who loves abundance, with increase. This also is vanity.* Material and sinful desires do not allow their prisoners to rest—ever.

Several years ago, I was invited to speak at a conference in New York. After speaking one evening, I retired to my room hoping to catch the last few innings of the World Series. Propped up on pillows, I sat on the bed with the remote in my hand, ready to enjoy America's favorite pastime at the high point of the season. Of course, being a typical male in possession of the remote control, I would surf other stations during commercial timeouts. During the transition between two innings, I surfed for a news station to alternate with the game.

As I flipped through the stations, I came across an image of a bare-breasted woman and quickly turned to the next channel. I was careful to change channels in the *opposite direction* every time I turned from the game after that experience. I am only too aware that opening the door a little gives sin the opportunity to overpower a person (see Gen. 4:7). But this is where a man's natural mind begins to mess with him. "Was that really what I thought it was? I didn't have my glasses on, so I can't be sure. Maybe I better turn back and make certain." But I did not follow that train of thought, because I know if a man sets little fires like that, he can soon be burning out of control. Give in to sexual lust, and you will discover a thirst that cannot be quenched. There is no rest for the wicked.

Have you ever been overtaken by road rage? I am convinced some people get in their cars and drive around with the sole intent of getting angry at another motorist. We live in a world with a surplus of anger. Anger is a *torrent (Prov. 27:4)*, difficult to calm once it has been stirred up (see Prov. 15:18); it leads to many transgressions (see Prov. 29:22). When we allow ourselves to become upset, we are like the waves of the sea, restless and agitated. If we allow ourselves to stay uptight, the anger builds and inevitably we will explode at someone—usually the wrong person, like our spouse or child. There is no rest for the wicked.

Greed will rob a person of God's peace. How is it

that wealthy people become so paranoid about their money that they feel they must hoard it or make more, even when they have more than they can reasonably spend in 20 lifetimes? Greed is an addiction, a terrible sickness that does not allow its host to rest.

We have met people who set goals for themselves they feel they have to reach before they can be happy. "As soon as I have my first million in the bank with a guaranteed income of $10,000 a month, I will kick back and enjoy life." But what happens if they reach those goals? They discover one million dollars is not enough to give them a real sense of security, satisfaction, or status—they need more. But once a person starts down that road, there is no termination point until death, and they lose it all in one fell swoop. For those who never reach the first million dollar mark, they are like donkeys chasing the carrot. Either one day they wake up to a joyous life totally independent of money, or they go on striving until they die and their ashes are thrown into the sea alongside the multimillionaire who died just as dissatisfied with life. There is no rest for the wicked.

Why is it that the wicked cannot find rest and peace? Because God is at war with wickedness. You do not have to be an expert strategist to know you cannot win a war against God. *There is no wisdom or understanding or counsel against the Lord (Prov. 21:30).* Fighting or even resisting God is a no-win situation, because if you seem to win today's battle, you have lost forever. Besides, why fight God when He loves you and He has your best interests at heart? To fight God is to fight against your own good.

RECOVERING THE STOLEN PEACE

If you have been robbed of your peace because of sinful desire or behavior, Scripture offers a wonderful hope. In Psalm 32, David describes in brilliant poetry how miserable he was while concealing a sin he had committed. He says, *When I kept silent, my bones grew old through my groaning all the day long (v. 3).* Endocrinologists (scientists who study endocrine glands) tell us that cortisol is a stress hormone the body produces to help us cope with situations mentally or emotionally difficult to resolve or endure. But what they have also discovered is too much cortisol can result in rapid aging, weight gain, and a loss of bone density leading to such ailments as osteoporosis. Wow! David was spot on regarding his symptoms *that his bones grew old.*

As long as David kept silent, holding his sin inside, it worked like a cancer against him—spiritually, emotionally, and physically. His mind and heart were that *troubled sea* Isaiah described. How did David find his way out of the storm?

I acknowledged my sin to You, and my iniquity I have not hidden. I said, "I will confess my transgressions to the Lord," and You forgave the iniquity of my sin (v. 5). I have known the misery of concealing a sin and the wonderful relief and joy to find God was eager to forgive me and restore me to complete fellowship with Himself, *He who covers his sins will not prosper, but whoever confesses and forsakes them will have mercy (Prov. 28:13).* David began his poem with these wonderful words, *Blessed is he whose transgression is forgiven, whose sin is covered (Ps. 32:1).*

If you have been a Christian for awhile, then you have heard these words many times: God has made provision for your sins and forgiveness is available. But even if you are reading this promise for the millionth time, you will find the energy of praise electrifies you so that with David you sing for the joy and happiness of knowing your sins are forgiven. What a relief! What a blessed transition from the troubled sea to peace like a river! What a wonderful thought that Jesus Christ sat down after purging our sins, that God the Father also rests in what Jesus accomplished on the cross, and that He invites us to also come and rest at the cross. There is rest and peace in Jesus' death for our sins and His resurrection into glorious life.

LAY YOUR BURDEN DOWN

I think it's time I told you how to experience God's perfect peace in the here and now. Remember, it does not have anything to do with the myths we exposed above. You will not find "Ten Easy Steps" to follow, or a secret plan or key to peace. If you want God's peace, and you have come to Him by way of Jesus Christ who changed your status from enemy of God to child of God, then what you must do is "be" in His peace. Does that sound too simplistic, too easy, too crazy?

I find so often Christians are begging God for gifts He has already given them. In fact, every gift God has for us is wrapped in one package; namely, Jesus Christ. But we are like Martha, *distracted with much serving . . . worried and troubled about many things (Luke 10:40-41).* What else could Martha have done, seeing she had so many people in her home? She could have joined Mary at Jesus' feet. Mary was in peace, in love, in a good place, and Jesus did not allow anyone to take that from her (see Luke 10:42). We are trying to *get* peace using Martha's method, which means keeping busy and doing everything we can under the sun. But like Martha, we are only getting worried and troubled. Join Mary and *be* in the peace that already surrounds you. Let your thoughts sink deep down in your soul where God has planted His peace. Breathe slow, deep breaths as you look for that inner peace of God.

When Jesus said, *"Peace I leave with you, My peace I give to you,"* He also said, *"Let not your heart be troubled, neither let it be afraid" (John 14:27).* Our hearts will *be* troubled, *be* afraid, or they will *be* at peace and in peace. You need to hear this again: you will *not* obtain peace even through your best efforts. You will not work your way into peace, think your way into peace, or even pray your way into God's peace. The Lord's peace is a reality you simply have to accept. We can rob ourselves of God's peace, but we cannot achieve God's peace by working for it.

Prayer

O Father,
Thank You for the wonderful peace of Jesus Christ.
Thank You, that You have forgiven our sins and
removed our guilt.
Thank You, Lord, that the war is over.
Now we breathe the rarified air of Your presence,
in a world that shimmers with Your radiance.

We inhale Your Spirit, and exhale praise;
we inhale forgiveness and exhale our petitions;
we inhale peace and exhale worry and anxiety.
Holy God, we lay down our arms and surrender.
Take over our lives with such force and completeness,
we have no more fight in us.
Calm the troubled sea of our minds,
speak peace to the wind and waves of our souls,
increase Your rule over our lives
until the peace of God that passes all understanding
guards our hearts and our minds in Christ Jesus.
Amen.

CHAPTER 7

Deposit Your Anxieties Here

> Be anxious for nothing, but in everything by
> prayer and supplication, with thanksgiving,
> let your requests be made known to God;
> and the peace of God, which surpasses all
> understanding, will guard your hearts and
> minds through Christ Jesus.
>
> (Phil. 4:6, 7)

One of my grandsons recently married and several months later finally decided to try to come up with a budget with his wife. When they computed their income against their expenditures, they realized that each month they will be $575 short on their fixed expenses, not including the food. Fortunately, my son and daughter-in-law enjoy having them in their home for dinner every night. But I sometimes wonder how young people survive these days, especially when housing costs are way beyond reach of the average couple, even when both the husband and wife are wage-earners.

The King James Version of Philippians 4:6 says, *Be careful for nothing*, which could be taken as, *Do not be full of care*, like Martha in Luke 10 when she was *wor-*

97

ried and troubled about many things (Luke 10:41). My heart goes out to people who cannot shut down the mechanisms in their brains that produce worry. Their thoughts and imaginations are constantly inventing potential future problems or catastrophes, and some of them are foolish enough to believe because the events they worry about never happen, then worrying must work. Their worries spoil life in the present by anticipating an unhappy future.

A woman who attends my church is an inveterate worrier. As she passed me at the exit one Sunday morning, I asked, "How are you this week?"

"Well everything is going very well for me," she responded.

I thought to myself, "At last! Now she can enjoy God's goodness for awhile."

But she looked distressed. I asked her another question, "Aren't you relieved everything is going well now?"

"No, I'm not," she responded. "I'm worried my life is too wonderful right now, so it can't possibly last, and I just know that pretty soon everything is going to fall apart." I suppose if you are a worrier then you have to worry about something.

Does worry solve problems? No, it merely circles them in an unending holding pattern. Worry does not lead to positive action, but more often results in inaction, either because worriers are afraid of doing the wrong thing. Or maybe it's because they devote so much time in their mental gyrations that every opportunity to do something of value passes them before they get out of the thinking stage. Worry and anxiety are destructive, rather than constructive mental processes. *Do not fret—it only causes harm (Ps. 37:8).*

Jesus once asked His disciples and the crowd sitting nearby, *"Which of you by worrying can add one cubit to his stature?" (Matt. 6:27).* Can worry add even one inch to your height, one minute to your life, or one charming feature to your personality? No! Worry is not the method by which we make positive changes in our lives, and it is totally useless regarding the things we cannot change, like our height. Anxiety burns precious mental reserves and wastes them; nothing in heaven or on earth is moved by anxious thoughts.

So what does Paul tell us to do about our anxieties and worries? *Be anxious for nothing*, he says in Philippians 4:6. This is Paul's general advice that lets us know it's possible and spiritually desirable to live a life free from anxiety. He spends the rest of this verse and the next explaining how it's possible to rid ourselves of anxiety.

TURN FEARS INTO PRAYERS

Since Paul explains what he knows about God setting us free from anxiety, we will take enough time to appreciate his counsel and begin to apply it. We might notice that he first suggests we take each anxious thought and instead of fretting over it, give it to God in the form of a prayer. Paul does not tell us merely to stop worrying because that is poor advice. If you are trying not to worry about something, then you are thinking of that thing. The more you think about it, the more it occupies your thoughts and stubbornly resists every effort not to think of it. If you try to wrestle with your worries, you will lose. Anxiety is fed by thought, so fighting anxiety feeds it as much as imagining its various scenarios.

We cannot fight worry successfully, so we must learn to acknowledge it and then let it go. When an anxious thought pops into your mind, greet it, then say good-bye. Acknowledge the thought has occurred, but tell it, "You will not imprison or define me. I see your point, but now I'm going to walk you to God and leave you with Him. He knows how to handle annoying pests like you." The next step is to make that anxious thought a rung in your ladder of prayer. Step on it to move closer to God.

> Have mercy on me, O Lord, for I am weak;
> O Lord, heal me, for my bones are troubled.
> My soul also is greatly troubled;
> But You, O Lord—how long?
>
> (Ps. 6:2-3)

When you wake up in the middle of the night, your mind and body agitated with disturbing thoughts, pray over each one as it intrudes into your mind. Most likely you will return to sleep quickly. Do not waste precious sleep time trying to work out insoluble problems. Sometimes it's helpful to have a pen and pad of paper nearby so you can write down each of your anxieties. Make a "wish list" for God. Tell Him, "Father, everything on my prayer list is something special I am asking You to do." This exercise is typically a very powerful mood changer.

My son-in-law, Greg, has said, "If I'm worried about one of my problems and God is also worried about it, then one of us is wasting time."

If God wants to worry about me, then I will enjoy myself and live carefree, because He can do a much better job than I can of managing and mending my life. If I am to *cast all my care upon Him (1 Pet. 5:7)*, what does that leave me to be anxious about? Paul said, *"Be anxious for nothing,"* but how much is *nothing*? Is. *nothing* a little bit of worry, a medium amount of fear, a lot of fretting? Wrong, wrong, and wrong! *Nothing* is not anything at all.

Ironically, when we are anxious, it is usually about *nothing;* that is, anxiety has to do with an imaginary fear. When you face real danger, you may feel terror, panic, or dread, but you do not feel anxiety. However, when you only *imagine* a future danger or you are uncertain about what events lie ahead and you dream up possible calamities or shudder that you don't know what is coming and it could be worse than anything you can imagine, then you feel anxious. So anxiety is about nothing, because the future is only an idea or a concept. If we are not to *boast about tomorrow* because we *do not know what a day may bring forth (Prov. 27:1),* then, as Jesus said, we certainly should not *worry about tomorrow, for tomorrow will worry about its own things. Sufficient for the day is its own trouble (Matt. 6:34).* Why worry about tomorrow when we may not even be here when tomorrow comes? (see Luke 12:20; James 4:13-14).

Of course, when Paul said we are to be anxious for nothing, he was saying we are not to let anything get us anxious—not tomorrow or anything that may occur tomorrow. We can think, we can plan, we can prepare, and we can pray about tomorrow, but we live and work in today. We have ruined or lost so many valuable moments because our brains were preoccupied with tomorrow rather than with God's splendor in the present. How true the line in Joseph Scriven's words from the old gospel hymn, "What a Friend We Have in Jesus":

> "O what peace we often forfeit,
>   O what needless pain we bear,
> All because we do not carry
>   Everything to God in prayer!"

I hope you picked up on that word *everything*, because that's the word Paul used regarding the things we make known to God: *in everything by prayer and supplication, with thanksgiving, let your requests be made known to God (Phil. 4:6).*

A SPIRITUAL EXERCISE?

Is there a practical way we can immediately apply Paul's teaching regarding anxiety? Can we find instant relief? Or do you suppose God would reveal a truth like this, so after years of self-discipline and painstaking effort we finally become holy enough to rid ourselves of our anxieties? God supplies to us everything we have and will ever need, by grace through His Son and His Spirit. Everything He has told us pertaining to our spiritual lives and godliness is ours right now. Are you ready to release some built-up pressure and let go of your anxiety?

Make yourself comfortable, sit up so your spine is straight, inhale slowly, relax your muscles, then slowly exhale. Place your hands on your lap with your palms up, but make a fist as if holding on to something. Imagine you carry all your anxieties in your hands. Begin to pray, "O God, hear my prayer." What anxious thought occurs? What are you worrying about? Tell God what is on your mind or troubling your heart. Let God know what you would like Him to do for you. Don't be specific—let God work out the details of how He will do *His* job. Go on to the next worry, and continue like this until you have completed your list and made your requests known.

For a moment, be still and observe the rhythm of your breath. People who are at rest breathe slowly. Each breath is a gift from God. Thank Him for the breath of life, for the good things He has given you, for the greatness of His mercy, and the fact that He loves you beyond any measure you could ever dream. As Paul said, *With thanksgiving, let your requests be made known to God (Phil. 4:6).*

Why is it at this point of our spiritual exercise we begin to become more conscious of God? For one reason, the pressing immediacy of anxious thoughts tend to block or override the awareness of God's less tangible Spirit. But another probable answer is in Psalm 100: *Enter into His gates with thanksgiving, and into His courts with praise. Be thankful to Him and bless His name (v. 4).* Our souls desire God, and in anxiety we become desperate for Him, but you will not get past His gates whining and complaining. The password to get you through the gates and into His courts is, "Thank You,

O God." Thanksgiving and praise open our awareness to God's presence in ways that petition and supplication do not. As far as complaining goes, as long
as you are talking about your problems over and over,
all you will be able to see or think about are those
problems; they become your fixation. Thanksgiving
liberates you from that obsession.

Now stretch out your arms, turn your hands over,
and open them, releasing your soul's grip on all those
anxieties you mentioned to God. Let every worry fall
away. Bring your hands back to your lap, turn them
over, and with your palms up, pray, "Lord, now I receive Your peace that surpasses all understanding.
Your peace now protects my heart and cares."

Can you see why we have failed to live in God's
peace? Our hands have been too full of the worries
and troubles of many things, and we haven't had
room to receive His grace. We have been clutching our
anxious thoughts until now.

Think of this spiritual exercise as an anxiety dump.
As soon as we move through this prayer, anxiety begins to melt away and the peace of God moves in to
take its place. Until now, we have forfeited peace that
could have been ours. We have carried unnecessary
sorrow and pain because we forgot to take *everything*
to God in prayer.

A FURTHER WORD ON GIVING THANKS

If we pray about everything with supplication *and
thanksgiving*, does that mean we give God thanks for
everything? I admit this seems like an outrageous

question; our reflexive answer is, "No!" I have a friend who lost an eye to cancer; how can he give thanks to God for that? I know a couple who lost their only child when she was three years old. How can they thank God for her illness and death? Will we give thanks to God that humans are being tortured, ethnic communities are being slaughtered, and starvation ravages millions of lives every day? What was Paul thinking?

I once sat in a Bible study where the minister took questions after his sermon. A woman asked him how we were supposed to give thanks to God when bad things happened to us? He turned to 1 Thessalonians 5:18, read the verse and said, "Notice that Paul says, '*in* everything give thanks,' he does not say '*for* everything.'"

A grizzled old man sitting in the back of the church shouted, "In Ephesians 5:20 he does!"

The minister had to smile and say, "Stay out of Ephesians for now."

If we cannot make a troubling verse go away, then we need to take a closer look at it to discover what it is God actually wants from us. One way to understand how it's possible to give thanks to God for everything is to surrender to a wisdom greater than our own. If *all things to work together for good to those who love God*—or *God works for the good*—(Rom. 8:28, NIV), then it's possible to learn to rest in God's higher wisdom and higher ways (see Is. 55:8-9). I do not mean that a loss in this life will result in a greater good in this life, or if God takes something from you it is to replace it with something better. We need to prepare ourselves for the possibility that the *good* for which all things work may not be in this lifetime. I can only make sense of my circumstances within a narrow scope of time, whereas God sees my life in the light of eternity.

I know God controls my life—as He does all things—and nothing happens to me but what God has allowed. The problem, of course, is that I cannot see far enough in time and space to grasp God's purpose in a specific situation. My concern is located within this moment of suffering and its immediate effect on me. My tendency is to drown in the moment and in my panic and forget the eternal. We are like the disciples who believed all hope was lost when Jesus died on the cross, when later they would give God eternal thanks for the crucifixion. Even on the cross—which was wrong, tragic, brutal, unjust, and unbearably painful—God was working out His eternal plan.

God does not expect us to say, "My child died, so that must be a good thing because the Bible says God makes all things work for good, and I am supposed to give thanks for everything." No, God expects us to weep, lament, and most likely complain bitterly. But eventually He calls us to a place of trust in which, like Job, we say, *"The Lord gave, and the Lord has taken away; Blessed be the name of the Lord"* (Job 1:21). But why would we even *want* to pray these words in the face of a tragedy from which we may never fully recover?

A tradition in Judaism says God has a blessing for everyone and for everything that happens. In *Fiddler on the Roof*, someone asks the village rabbi, "Is there a blessing for the czar?"

He answers, "Of course there is a blessing for the czar." Then he intones, "May God bless and keep the czar . . . far away from here!"

In *The Journey Home: Discovering the Deep Spiritual Wisdom of Jewish Tradition*, Lawrence Hoffman explains that the human spirit is driven by an urge to find meaning in everything. Therefore the use of the blessing not only transforms the nature of a thing, but it alerts the person who pronounces the blessing to look for what is holy in everything. We could say the blessing serves as a reminder to look for God's gift, His grace in every event and circumstance.

If we look at everything as a gift, then everything matters and has a meaning. We do not act like suffering and loss are unimportant or meaningless, but we give thanks to God for even the heartbreaking experiences, and in that way connect them with God. The practice of giving thanks will prove to be spiritually beneficial, even when we do not feel thankful. What happens if we do not look for God's gift of grace in every thing? What if we cannot take even the thought, "O God, I hate this terrible loss in my life" to God? Then we cannot connect it to God and we are lost.

Not as the World Gives

People who live apart from Jesus Christ have difficulty trying to understand the wonderful peace God gives His children in the most difficult circumstances. We get accustomed to hearing that following a tragedy, people who witnessed the devastation or were victims of it are immediately rushed off to psychologists and counselors for their mental health's sake. People are not able to sort mentally through, resolve, and adjust to these overwhelming circumstances. The term post-traumatic stress disorder is being increasingly applied to a greater number of distressing conditions where it may not always apply. We've almost gotten to the point where it's an expected result rather than a rare but serious disorder.

But some believers have come to a place in their journey with God that even senseless tragedy cannot push them to despair. Not long ago I received a message from a woman who provides hospice care for terminal patients. She wanted to tell me about a lady who will soon pass away. Her body is emaciated and has withered to 70 pounds. But the whole time she was in the hospital, doctors and nurses would visit her room so *she* could encourage them, because she radiated the joy and love of Jesus Christ. She is living in a *peace that passes all understanding*, a *peace the world cannot give*. The hospice worker wanted me to know her health care professionals have never seen anyone like her and are deeply moved by the light she shines.

In John 14:27, Jesus said, *"Peace I leave with you, My peace I give to you; not as the world gives do I give to you. Let not your heart be troubled, neither let it be afraid."* How does the world give? Superficially. The world gives clichés to broken hearts; it does what it can to relieve the symptoms. The world puts bandages on mortal wounds. Like the leaders of Israel in Jeremiah's day, the world has *healed the hurt of My people slightly, saying, "Peace, peace!" When there is no peace (Jer. 6:14).*

Jeremiah was referring to Israel's religious leaders—prophets and priests—in the above quote (see Jer. 6:13). People, even believers, who offer their suffering family and friends simplistic solutions to complex problems are healing their wounds only slightly or superficially. To hand suffering, starving, anxiety-ridden people clichés rather than deep-level help, to give them words rather than food, to quote Scripture rather than *rejoice with those who rejoice* and *weep with those who weep (Rom. 12:15),* to say, "Peace, peace!" rather than walk with them, is the same superficial help we get from the world.

I can imagine you saying, "Chuck, you're complicating the issue at hand. If we simply do exactly what the Bible says—*Be anxious for nothing*—then everything will resolve itself through God's help. I will not argue that point with you, but I will say if you only give mere words to people who are in need, then you are not doing enough. The Bible is clear that words—even good words, biblical words—are not enough. James said, *If a brother or sister is naked and destitute of daily food, and one of you says to them, "Depart in peace, be warmed and filled," but you do not give them the things which are needed for the body, what does it profit? (James 2:15-16).*

John echoes the same truth when he says, *But whoever has this world's goods, and sees his brother in need, and shuts up his heart from him, how does the love of God abide in him?*

My little children, let us not love in word or in tongue, but in deed and in truth (1 John 3:17-18).

The world gives superficially and inadequately. Because the world cannot dispense God's grace, it will never give sufferers all they need. Our bodies may need food, clothing, and medicine, but our souls need God. What the world gives is perishable and has a brief shelf life, whereas the gift of Jesus *endures to eternal life (John 6:27).* The world gives illusions, false promises, and false hopes, but the promise of God is real and reliable.

So for you to give up your anxiety, you will have to give up your illusions—that your family cannot manage without you, that you can bring the universe under your control, that you can meet every expectation placed on you no matter how outrageous, that by worrying you can add an inch to your height or a year to your life, or that you are the Messiah and must save the world. As long as you hang on to your worldly illusions, you will not be free from anxiety.

HEART FAILURE AND MENTAL BREAKDOWNS

Jesus described cosmological upheaval and human reaction when He talked about events that would precede His return. *Men's hearts failing them from fear and the expectation of those things which are coming on the earth, for the powers of heaven will be shaken (Luke 21:26).* Heart disease is one price we pay for clinging to our anxieties. But the promise of Scripture is that the peace of God would guard our hearts. And not only our hearts but also our minds as well. Imagine God standing guard over your mind so no matter what you see or hear, His peace never leaves you.

Isaiah knew something about God's peace:

> You will keep him in perfect peace,
> Whose mind is stayed on You,
> Because he trusts in You.
> Trust in the Lord forever,
> For in YAH, the Lord, is everlasting
>   strength.
>
> (Is. 26:3-4)

A mind stayed or fixed on God will be a mind at peace. Fixate on your problem and it will get worse. Focus attention on yourself, and you will fall into despair. But turn your eyes toward God and you will discover a God who fights for you while you repose in His perfect peace (see 2 Chr. 20:12-15).

Prayer

Heavenly Father,
we grab hold of Your promise,
because it is the salvation that will keep us
from drowning in despair,
giving up all hope,
or becoming *victims* of life's hardships
rather than *victors* through Jesus.
Have You really promised to *guard our hearts
and minds*
with a *peace that surpasses all understanding?*
We have no way to thank You adequately
for Your generous care.

So we will do what we can;
we will give up our anxieties and trust You;
we will let go of our worries and praise You;
we will keep our minds stayed on You,
and through Jesus Christ, enjoy Your perfect peace,
both now and forevermore, world without end.
Amen.

CHAPTER 8

Using Prayer as an Antidepressant

Why are you cast down, O my soul?
And why are you disquieted within me?
Hope in God;
For I shall yet praise Him,
The help of my countenance and my God.

(Ps. 42:5)

THE PSALM AS "POEM"

Poetry is meant to be read and reflected on in a different way from other forms of writing. I would not be surprised if we used a different part of our brain while reading poetry than reading a newspaper article or textbook. Poems ignore the normal conventions of word usage, phrasing, and grammar to force us to look at people, objects, and events in a new or unusual way. Poems are meant to make us feel the power of a thought, event, experience, or truth.

When my children were small they would sometimes beg me to read to them the poem, "Little Boy Blue" by Eugene Field. Inevitably they would dis-

113

solve into tears before I reached the last line. Why did
they enjoy hearing the tragic pathos of this short story
told in poetry? Probably for the same reason ancient
Greeks and Romans went to the theater to weep at the
tragedies of playwrights. In part, it's due to the way
tragedy told in an artful way helps us discover how
deep our feelings penetrate into our soul. I doubt the
bare story of "Little Boy Blue" would have had the
same effect on my kids as did the poem. You may say
inanimate toys are incapable of providing eternal and
loyal friendship, but even at a young age my children
fully grasped the meaning behind the words:

> And as he was dreaming, an angel song
> Awakened our Little Boy Blue,—
> Oh, the years are many, the years are long,
> But the little toy friends are true!

Psalms 42 and 43 are poems, and they are meant to
be read together. What is their theme? It is an unhappy soul looking for God, and the structure of the
poems reinforces the theme through repetition. The
poems keep returning to the words *shakah—to sink
down, be bowed down, depress*—and *hamah—to cry out* or
moan. Both Hebrew words are used poetically to ex-
press strong feelings. In these poems, they give expression to the poet's despair and inner turmoil. In
modern terms we might ask, "Why are you so depressed? Why are you riddled with anxiety?"

By inserting a refrain three times in the poems—
42:5-6, 11; and 43:5—David shows us how they are to
be read. In Psalm 42:1-5 he describes his need, deep

sorrow, and what provoked it. Nevertheless, under-neath his intense sadness, David counsels his soul to hope in God and he can envision a future time of praise for the help of God's countenance; that is, His face or presence (42:5).

In the next movement, verses 6-11, David describes his soul's experience of being overwhelmed with mis-ery, and again he uses metaphorical language—God's *waves and billows (42:7)*. He concludes this section with his refrain and clinging to hope.

Psalm 43 dispenses the metaphors of deer and wa-terfalls and goes straight into a courtroom where David pleads for God to deliver him from the oppres-sion of his enemy. Finally, in verses 3 and 4, David comes to the solution to his despair. Now he can com-plete his poetic journey by singing the refrain one last time with confident hope he will appear before God.

Now that we know the poetic structure David used to describe his experience, we can move in for a closer look. There are lessons in these poems I do not want you to miss if you suffer with depression. First, Psalm 42 opens with a simile that will make sense if we pose the following question: Water is to a deer as *what* is to *what*? Water is to a deer as God is to the poet's thirsty soul. From the very first lines we learn he is desper-ately trying to find his way to God, that he *needs* an encounter with God—*When shall I come and appear be-fore God? (42:2)*. Through these two poems, David will be searching for the answer.

Metaphors can be helpful in *reframing* the way we look at ourselves and our emotions. For example, it is easy for people who are in despair to say, "I cannot feel

God's presence and I believe He has abandoned me because I am a bad person." But if we adopt David's metaphor, we make an important move away from surplus guilt to intense desire, *My soul thirsts for God (42:2)*. We can practically walk our way through Psalm 42 using metaphors like stepping stones. For example, David explains next he has been on a *liquid diet, My tears have been my food day and night (42:3)*. His sorrow is indeed liquid: *I pour out my soul within me (42:4)*.

In arranging the poem as he did, David introduced ideas in the first section he returned to in the second section. For example, he discovered memory could work both against him and for him. In 42:4, he recalled previous worship experiences that included joy, praise, and feasting. But in 42:6, he made use of his memory (42:4) to connect with God while far away from the temple, knowing God is not bound by space or time (42:6).

Let's look at another parallel between the two sections. *Day and night* tears of verse three corresponds to the *daytime mercy* and *night*, a song of verse 8. Here is a glimmer of hope, as if David broke the surface of the water to catch a breath of air. By the way, the headwaters of the Jordan River begin at Mount Hermon, far to the north of Jerusalem (42:6). Is it possible David sat near a waterfall and realized how His soul was tortured by a torrent of rushing water? The *deep calling unto deep* could easily be the darkness of deep water echoing the darkness in which his soul was drowning. Think about this: if David's soul could thirst for God, it could also be drowned by God's waves and billows (42:1-2, 7).

Another parallel has to do with the question that will not go away; David's enemies raise it: *Where is your God? (42:3, 10)*. The enemy's oppression and taunting are intensified by the fact they assault him with the same question he has been asking himself. By mixing his speech in 43:1—is the enemy a *nation* or an *unjust man?*—David leaves open the possibility the enemy is not literal, but rather that circumstances or his mental state attack his soul. Either way, he is not looking for help *from* God, but for God to *be* his help.

One more parallel and we will move on. Did you notice the subtle changes between verses 5 and 11? The two verses are almost exact, so you have to read them carefully. In verse 5 David said he would praise God for the help of *His* countenance, but in verse 11 he says, *The help of* my *countenance* then adds the words, *and my God.* God's countenance is the power that changes our countenance, *The Lord lift up His countenance upon you, and give you peace (Num. 6:26)*. In the previous psalm, David rejoiced because God made him strong in integrity by setting David before His face forever (41:12). To be face-to-face with God is the language of encounter, and this is the theme of these desperate poems.

LIFE IN THE PRESSURE COOKER

We live in a stress-filled society. Although God created us with a remarkable capacity to respond to the demands of the world around us, I sometimes wonder if we were made to live at the speed our lives currently travel. Were we meant to deal with as much information as we are bombarded with every day or try to manage as many challenges at one time as we are expected to resolve in a week, month, or year? I do not wonder, however, that only electronic systems get easily overloaded; even our body's central nervous system is overwhelmed. One of the by-products of living in a society such as ours is a high rate of depression and anxiety.

Not wishing to add more items to your list of "Things that make me want to scream," I cannot help but think inescapable responsibilities, for some reason, have become more stressful than what I can remember them being only a few years ago. For example, we have a huge number of interpersonal relationships through our mobility, a growing number of ways to keep in touch, global networks of business, and a multiplicity of families through divorce and remarriage. The latter is a fairly recent configuration that increases the complexity of knowing to whom we are related, how we are related, and what is expected from us within those relationships. When it comes to our careers, most of us are aware our to-do list will outlive us, the demands on our performance or production are greater than we can meet, and deadlines are killing us. Sometimes Christians have the added pressure of being the only believer on the factory floor, construction site, or office suite.

What about problems that arise from neighbors who either nag you about your children or terrify you with theirs? Every street seems to have a neighborhood grouch, and every association has at least one spy who drives up and down the streets checking whose driveway has an oil stain and who left their garage door open or their trash cans out. Woe to the father who asks the teenager next door to quiet down the party so he and his family can sleep, the single mother who argues with the association that she should not be fined because she let the petunias in front of her house die, or the elderly woman who answers her door to a fast-talking roof repairman who tells her the tiles on her roof need to be sprayed with a fire retardant! Best to give in to the oppression and abuse because no one today has time to fight all these battles—except for the resident grouch driving the neighborhood to check on us!

There is no end to marital challenges, pesky and unexpected financial demands, work issues, domestic concerns, and social ills. For most of us, our lives are so delicately balanced that one or two hiccups could throw the whole system out of control, and a month later we will be standing at a freeway on ramp with a sign that says, "Will work for food." All these pressures accumulate in intensity and create greater distress as life rolls on, threatening our sanity, our faith, and our health.

Oh yes, we hear about another pressure every day. The issues of diet and how we are going to kill, disable, or mentally incapacitate ourselves by eating the wrong foods. The problem is the right food yesterday suddenly becomes the wrong food today, and yesterday's healthy diet is today's killer. Yet you do not have to be overly worried about your diet because the over-abundance of cortisol—a stress hormone—in our systems is causing us to gain weight and age rapidly, while our adrenal glands either burn out or wear our hearts down to nothing, which is what is happening to those of us who live with too much stress for too long. Whew!

Some people suffer from a strange phenomenon which is neither manic nor depressive, but is simple boredom. They cannot make themselves feel anything; happiness or sorrow, peace or fear, good or bad. We refer to this condition as "a case of the blahs," but it can be much more serious to the person who is stuck in life's monotonous grind. Then there are the disorders over which we have little or no control, such as diabetes, Crohn's disease, bipolar disorder, obsessive-compulsive disorder, and depression. These conditions do not necessarily have causes that result from poor decisions, but are rooted in the physiology of our bodies or the neurology of our brains. "Do not ask me why," my son might say, "I am just depressed." We have been boxed-in by life or betrayed by our bodies.

I can understand why people turn to alcohol, drugs, affairs, or why they would want to end their lives. They are either self-medicating, coping, or giving up. If people are going to survive, they will have to choose their crutch. Sadly, the crutches people tend to grab are often self-destructive. I know a man who was a brilliant engineer in an earlier period of his life. Back then, he had no need of God; his intellect was his crutch. But after suffering a stroke, he lost his great mental wealth and power, and he has become fearful, childish, and in need of others to feed him and care for him. His crutch gave out. He chose poorly.

Is God just a crutch to believers? No, that is not *all* God is to us, but no doubt among all the other wonderful things, He *is* a crutch, and the very best available to the human race. To admit Jesus Christ is a crutch is not to admit to weakness, but to confess in a time of flood, any intelligent person will seek higher ground. As the psalmist said, *When my heart is overwhelmed; lead me to the rock that is higher than I (Ps. 61:2).* So if you ask whether God is my crutch, I say, "Yes! I lean on Him every day, and He has never let me down."

Apart from a crutch, few people can keep pace in our society without succumbing to depression or another mental disorder or breakdown. While we might be tempted to worry about the growing rate of adults diagnosed and treated for depression, mental health institutions have a greater concern for the growing number of high school and college students suffering with depression. In a time of life that is supposed to be filled with fun, adventure, optimism, and idealism, young people are feeling as overwhelmed as their parents by demands imposed on them. And what kind of life do they have to look forward to once they graduate and move into their careers? Not only more of the same, but even greater pressure and more demands.

TUNNEL VISION

Have you ever wondered how a person struggling with depression can see the beauty of a sunset, hear a compelling piece of music, spend quality time with a good friend, and yet still be unhappy? If you remind a person in depression they have blessings and not everyone is able to enjoy eyes to see, ears to hear, legs, arms, and the ability to taste good food, you'll probably get from them a look as if to say, "There's no use in trying to explain to you what I feel because you will never get it." Depression is not always triggered by specific events and is hardly ever resolved by a specific event or experience. It's a serious and lasting disorder, and I would go so far as to say if you thought you were depressed and received good news that snapped you out of it, you were probably not depressed.

If you have never known depression, have you experienced heart-rending grief, the kind of deep and agonizing pain you feel when someone you love dies? We can compare our grief to the pain Jesus felt in the Garden of Gethsemane, when He told His disciples, *"My soul is exceedingly sorrowful, even to death"* (Mark 14:34).

Depression, like grief, drains all the color out of the world, all the taste out of life, all the enjoyment out of friendships, and all the hope out of the heart. Clinical depression often occurs when a person's brain is not able to utilize the chemicals that produce positive and secure feelings. No matter what their situation in life, they will not feel peace, joy, or comfort, but only despair. A lot of money and possessions, good looks and good health, or intelligence and significant achievements cannot lift a person out of depression.

Depression also interferes with a person's ability to see beyond the small circumference of his own mind and situation. Problems appear to be unavoidable, universal, and they look like they will last forever. If you cannot look around you for some kind of escape or solution, and you cannot see any possibility of your situation changing in the future, then all you have left is a feeling of permanent and stubborn misery; you are hopeless.

I am amazed how well David and the other poets who wrote the psalms—not to mention Job—understood depression. A cast-down soul is a good way to describe depression. The soul descends into a dark pit, which was close to the grave, and shared all its characteristics (see Ps. 40:2; 88:6). Cast down, and unable to struggle to its feet on its own, David's soul fought a hopeless battle against a despair that he could not understand, which is why he asked, *Why are you cast down, O my soul?*

David had a plan. First, he would get God's attention, then he would say to Him, *"Why have You forgotten me? Why do You cast me off? Why do I go mourning because of the oppression of the enemy?"* Then, I'm not sure whether David came up with a strategy for getting himself into God's presence or if a new and better idea suddenly came to him, but he shifted from complaining to making a request:

> Oh, send out Your light and Your truth!
> Let them lead me; Let them bring me to
>   Your holy hill
> And to Your tabernacle.
> Then I will go to the altar of God,
> To God my exceeding joy;
> And on the harp I will praise You,
> O God, my God.
>
> (Ps. 43:3-4)

Perhaps unknowingly, David had come upon the way that led out of the pit, out of the dark maze and tunnel of despair and into God's presence.

When I read David's words, *Let them lead me,* I immediately ask, "Where?" Where does David wish to go? Where does he want God's light and truth to take him? To God's holy hill and to tabernacle. With this request we return to the place we started, with a soul thirsting for God. David was overwhelmed by his circumstances and the sorrow they engendered. But God was not overwhelmed, and He alone was able to deal with David's external and internal situation.

Look at how David developed these two verses. Follow the progress David makes as he moves geographically through the text, to God's holy hill, then on to His tabernacle, and finally at His altar. Why did David stop at the altar? What was his objective and how was the altar the end of his journey? In case the answer is not obvious to you already, I will explain. The altar was the place where anyone could go, no matter how guilty, sinful, unworthy, or deserving of punishment. Sins were atoned for and forgiveness was dispensed at the altar. God opened His arms to receive everyone who came to the altar, even His prodigal sons and daughters. And what the altar was to Old Testament religion, the cross of Jesus Christ is for New Testament believers.

Do you feel you are worthless? Are you convinced your sin disqualifies you from enjoying a relationship with God? Do you think you cannot find a place close to God? Well, think again, because *even the sparrow has found a home* at God's altar *(Ps. 84:3)*. If a sparrow—

which the Bible uses as a symbol of something of little value—can build a nest for her young at God's altar, then you will certainly find love, forgiveness, and acceptance there. After all, our Lord said, *Do not fear therefore; you are of more value than many sparrows (Matt. 10:31).*

Why are you cast down, O my soul? Why so depressed and anxious? *Hope in God,* because in answer to your prayer, His light and truth are there, and they will lead you to the holy hill and the cross of Jesus and onward into the heart of God.

Do Not Put Your Trust in Princes

How did David counsel his soul? What advice did he give to his soul in the refrain? He told his soul to *hope in God.* If you put your hope anywhere else, then it is misplaced.

> Do not put your trust in princes,
> Nor in a son of man, in whom there is no
>   help.
> His spirit departs, he returns to his earth;
> In that very day his plans perish.
> Happy is he who has the God of Jacob for
>   his help,
> Whose hope is in the Lord his God.
>   (Ps. 146:3-5)

How many times I have put my hope in man only to be disappointed. I have been lied to, cheated, deceived, and defrauded so many times I am embarrassed to speak of those mistakes. But still, when new problems occur, my first instinct is to look around for someone who can help me. I suppose most of us have learned the hard way *it is better to put your trust in the Lord than to put your confidence in man (Ps. 118:8).*

Not only do friends and sponsors fail to come through, but we also have to deal with those relentless enemies. One of the great social sicknesses of the human race is someone is always prepared to profit from disaster, to prey upon people who have suffered misfortune. Before any world relief organization could get to Sumatra after the devastating tsunami in 2004, evil soul merchants had come from other Asian and a few European countries to kidnap recently orphaned children for the sex slave industry.

People can be so heartless and evil. A plane crashes and an attorney makes his way among surviving family members in the airport, handing out business cards and telling them how much money he can get them from a lawsuit against the airline. If you get behind on your bills, a loan shark will contact you, promising you relief with a loan he knows you cannot pay off, but he will walk away with your wedding ring and other valuable jewelry or possessions you own. Unethical realtors arrive when your house is threatened with foreclosure. They warn you of the problems you will face if you lose your good credit, and they volunteer to take your house off your hands. Then they rent out your home, ride out the foreclosure, and afterward enjoy the income from the rental and your credit is destroyed in the process.

We can add to this list people who promise miracle

cures, whether in Latin American clinics or divine healing crusades. No matter what the disease, someone will guarantee a remedy to fix you right up. People who suffer or have a dying child are so desperate, they are willing to accept the flimsiest of promises on the outside chance they may see a miracle. Rather than curing anyone, the various snake oil salesmen line their pockets with the plunder of misfortune. Given the fact of these enemies, you begin to wonder if you can trust anyone.

David counseled his soul to hope in God. In essence, he said, "O my soul, redirect your attention. Look away from your problem, it will only cast you down; look away from others, they will let you down; look away from your feeble arms and meager funds, they will bring you down. Put your hope in God and look toward His holy hill. If you look from your weakness to God's strength, then you will rediscover His great love for you, His power over your world, and that He is watching you and listening to your prayer."

DO NOT TRUST YOURSELF

David's cold soul replied, "If God is in control and He loves me, then why am I in this state? Why hasn't God helped me already?" In fact, these questions are implied in David's cry for help, *Why do I go mourning because of the oppression of the enemy? (Ps. 42:9).*

I am convinced God wants to work through my problems with me, but I have also learned He rarely joins me before I get to the end of myself. Only when

I come to the absolute limit of my ability and resources, when I know I can do nothing more, and I admit the challenge is beyond me, do I see God begin to work.

You see, I tend to be incurably self-righteous. My mind is always telling me if I apply myself sufficiently and diligently, I can resolve every issue that confronts me. I have a lot of confidence in myself, which has at times exacerbated my problems. Like the "glory hog" outfielder who rushes to catch every fly ball, we love the glory. Of course all God has to do is allow the problem to return, perhaps with even greater force, and we are driven to our knees again. Do you suppose God sometimes allows our circumstances to get as severe as they can become so we quickly come to the end of ourselves and place a real confidence and trust in Him?

David asked, *Why are you cast down, O my soul?* If I were to ask the same question, it is very likely my soul could come back at me with the answer, "Because I've been trying to make it on my own, trying to solve all these problems myself, trying to carry these burdens with nothing but my own strength. I'm depressed because I am exhausted and cannot take another step."

A SPIRITUAL POWER TOOL

Typically, depressed people are hopeless, not only because they cannot find any solution within themselves or coming from the world around them, but they have trouble hoping in God because they think of themselves as worthless, stupid, and evil. Depression is often intensified by severe self-loathing.

I mentioned that David used a powerful device to help him deal with his depression, and here it is: he spoke to his soul. Look at the number of times in these two psalms that David referred to his soul as if it were a person separate from himself. He was talking to himself, but by addressing his soul, he found a way to step back from his situation as if he could watch his soul struggle without being engaged or trapped in that struggle himself. If you are depressed, try this simple exercise:

Look at yourself, not through your own mind, but as if you were on the other side of a counselor's office or looking at another person. What do you see? Someone who is oppressed with sadness and confusion; someone who feels totally unloved and unlovable. Someone who has no emotional support, no hope, no one who understands their misery. You see someone who is afraid and alone. Do you feel any sympathy or compassion for that sad, broken person? That is how God feels toward you when He looks on you in your broken condition. You can only feel like a failure or a bad person. But if you stand back and talk to your soul like David did, then you will have more confidence when you bring it to God because your heart will not condemn you (see 1 John 3:21).

Look at yourself in this same detached way, but as if you were looking through God's eyes. What does God see? He sees His child in pain, drowning in unhappiness. He asks, "Why are you sad, My child?"

You answer, "Because I am unclean."

And do you know what God says to you? He says, "Do not call 'unclean' what I have cleansed." God loves His children, even when they have injured themselves through disobedience. He is neither pleased nor glorified when we wallow in guilt. God's grace is the power that removes guilt and tells us we are valuable to Him. God wants to *rejoice over you with singing (Zech. 3:17)*, but your *harp is turned to mourning* and your *flute to the voice of those who weep (Job 30:31)*.

If you can look at your soul with compassion rather than self-loathing, then you will begin to realize the magnitude of God's love for you and that He has chosen you for Himself.

Would you return to the altar with me for one moment? We saw that it is the place of acceptance and encounter, but there is so much more. Everything changed for David at the altar, because he met God—his exceeding joy—there. Isn't that a wonderful contrast? His soul went from total despair to exceeding joy. This transformation called for a song of celebration, so David tuned his harp to praise (see Ps. 43:4). All we need for robust praise and true worship is the altar, a harp, and the voice of a soul rescued from despair.

> Why are you cast down, O my soul?
> Why are you disquieted within me?
> Hope in God; for I shall yet praise Him,
> The help of my countenance and my God.
>   (Ps. 42:11)

Prayer

Father, we will praise You forever
for the concern You show for our souls.
We live in a cauldron of pressure,
yet it is the crucible that refines us.
We bring to you the pressures of our lives
and the distress that they have created in our minds;
we bring to You our despair and sadness,
our misery and depression,
our doubt and cast-down souls.
Thank You for Your patience while we struggle on
our own.
Thank You for the cross where we can reconnect with
Your presence.
Thank You for Your light and truth
that guide us back to the safety of Your house.
Please continue to deliver us from all our enemies—
both the internal and external forces that assail us.
We have no strength but You,
no crutch besides You,
no hope other than You.
We will yet praise You,
the help of our countenance and our God.
Through the name and goodness of Your Son,
Jesus Christ.
Amen.

CHAPTER 9

Good News
for Troubled Hearts

Let not your heart be troubled; you believe
in God, believe also in Me.

(John 14:1)

The warm light of flickering torches revealed the anxious faces of the disciples who sat around the table staring at Jesus. They would soon pepper Him with questions, like, "How can we know the way to where You are going?"; "Would you show us the Father?"; "How will You reveal Yourself to us and not to the world?" Jesus had created an agitation that stirred them up by telling them, *"Little children, I shall be with you a little while longer. You will seek Me; and as I said to the Jews, 'Where I am going, you cannot come,' so now I say to you" (John 13:33).*

He had also dropped the bombshell on Peter, *"The rooster shall not crow till you have denied Me three times" (John 13:38).* There was little Jesus could say afterward to allay their anxious concern.

These men had committed themselves to Jesus and the kingdom of God which He had promised to them.

In the words of Peter, they had *left all* to follow Jesus (see Mark 10:28). Now Jesus was talking about leaving them. What would they do without Him? Their lives revolved around His life, their future was dependent on His promise, their beliefs and worldview were derived from His teaching. How could they survive without Him? We are not surprised that their hearts were troubled, but we are shocked that given this context Jesus would say, *"Let not your heart be troubled."*

A NIGHT OF BAD NEWS

Our hearts are troubled when someone we love is close to death or we learn a family member or friend has died. We can feel their loss in the deepest place of our souls, evoking unanswerable questions: "How will we to manage without her?"; "What will we do?"; "Will the empty place they leave in our lives ever be filled?"; "Will the pain ever go away?" The disciples were suddenly forced to come to grips with these torturous issues the night Jesus told them He was going away and they could not go with Him.

When someone we love is suffering and we do not know why, and we cannot alleviate their grief or pain, we suffer too. Our hearts break when a friend cries and says, "Oh, I am in so much pain right now." Jesus, whom the disciples loved more than any other person in the world, told them earlier that His soul was troubled, creating conflict within Him regarding how He should pray (see John 12:27). A while later, the disciples could see He was troubled in spirit, and He spoke with such sadness that their hearts were filled with sorrow (see John 13:21-22; 16:6).

We are guilt-ridden afterward and filled with regret when we fail or offend a friend, abandon them when running from danger, betray them by divulging a secret, or set them up to be hurt. We don't want to hear from our friend that he does not trust us. When Jesus told His disciples, *"Assuredly, I say to you, one of you will betray Me,"* they became *"exceedingly sorrowful, and each of them began to say to Him, 'Lord, is it I?'"* (Matt. 26:21-22).

We naturally panic when we receive news that a huge change is about to take place in our lives that leaves our future uncertain. If we have thrown our whole life into a project and are completely dependent on its success but discover one night it will be scrapped, we are devastated and find our outlook bleak. Similarly the disciples' minds were thrown into chaos when Jesus announced they had come to the end of their journey with Him and would travel into the future on their own.

When someone we trust or depend on—like a parent, supervisor, or employer—begins to make obscure or confusing remarks to us; when we know that something important is at stake, but we cannot comprehend what is happening or what it means; when every explanation we receive about a difficult prospect creates even more confusion, we find ourselves worried and frustrated. Most people feel intense fear if suddenly their lives turn into chaos or something they believed they could always rely on goes out of control. So we can imagine that the disciples' heads began to swim that last night with Jesus when He spoke in figurative language and could not speak clearly to them about the Father (see John 16:25).

Any one of the above situations can trouble a human heart, but when we put them all together, we wonder how the disciples could compose themselves and not crumble to the floor in tears. One disturbing piece of information followed another, until the disciples were quite overwhelmed. It was at this point of critical mass that Jesus said, *"Let not your heart be troubled."*

EMPTY WORDS?

Christian friends, even Christian counselors, can be annoying. They may offer cheap advice or pious instruction meant to be encouraging, but which instead has a hollow ring. You lose your job and you are told, "Don't worry, God has something better for you." A close relative dies, and you are told, "Don't grieve, she is in a better place." You are struggling to survive a period of deep depression, only to have someone at church tell you, "Smile!" or "Cheer up, brother. God is on the throne!"

We might want to classify these people with Job's friends whom he referred to as *worthless physicians* and *miserable comforters (Job 13:4; 16:2)*, as if to say, "You are killing the patient you are supposed to cure and discouraging the troubled heart you are supposed to lift." We would like to say, "I am not your *brother*" to the person who says, "Smile, brother!" Job, however, bluntly told his friends, *Your platitudes are proverbs of ashes (Job 13:12),* and he asked them, *How then can you comfort me with empty words . . . ? (Job 21:34).* Anthony De Mello said such words were "absolutely true and totally worthless."*

During a season of severe turmoil, the shallow advice of well-meaning people can range from ridiculous to totally worthless. To tell a person who is grieving the death of their closest friend, mentor, and Savior, *"Let not your heart be troubled"* seems like utter nonsense. The disciples must have wanted to respond, "How could my heart *not* be troubled in light of what You've just said?!" But you see, whether a person's simple counsel is worthless or helpless sometimes depends completely on who offers the counsel.

One day Jesus crossed paths with a widow on her way to a graveyard to bury her only son. Luke tells us that *He had compassion on her, and said to her, "Do not weep" (Luke 7:13).* Perhaps He saw in her a resemblance to His own mother's broken heart. In the Greek text, Jesus spoke only two words to her, *"Weep not."* The simple command was all she needed to hear from Him. Any other caregiver who had any wisdom or compassion would tell her, "Go ahead and weep. This is part of the grief process, and you must continue to move through this terrible pain." But Jesus could do something about life and death.

Our response to simple commands depends on who speaks the command. If Jesus tells you, "Don't cry," then you do not need to go on crying because what-

---

* Anthony De Mello, *Awareness: The Perils and Opportunities of Reality* (New York, NY: Doubleday, 1990), 158.

ever broke your heart will be resolved, reversed, or re-
paired. The first lesson we need to learn is the comfort
Jesus gives to troubled hearts is like that of no other
friend, counselor, or pastor. God's power and grace
are released in the words Jesus speaks. Take confidence in His reassurance.

FURTHER LESSONS IN REASSURANCE

Another difference between Jesus and our friends
who offer shallow advice is that Jesus did not only
say, *"Let not your heart be troubled,"* but He went on to
give the disciples reasons or means to rely on His
counsel. For example, He helped them extend to Him
the faith they had in God, by saying, *"You believe in
God, believe also in Me" (John 14:1).* It was not just the
bare command that Jesus gave the disciples, but
along with the command He gave them the means;
namely, trust.

If we read the words of Jesus too quickly, we might
miss a critical application for our own time in history.
When evangelical Christians talk—or argue—about
faith in God, much of the time they are referring to beliefs or specific doctrines. If a Christian thinks that believing a doctrine about God or Jesus is the most important key to a spiritual life, then the chief concern is
to be right or to believe the correct doctrine. But troubled hearts are not consoled or mended by believing
in correct doctrines. Read carefully what Jesus says
here because He is not talking about believing in *doctrines*, but believing in *Persons*: Himself and the Father. The difference is between believing a set of be-

liefs and trusting our Creator and His Son, who is our Savior.

The disciples have traveled and lived with Jesus; they know Him. Now He is telling them, "I realize you do not understand what I have been telling you, so I am asking you to trust Me. Trust Me in the way you have learned to trust God." Jesus' encouragement is also a challenge. He is asking the disciples to trust His wisdom, power, and love. He is asking them to look past the darkness of the hour, knowing He is obeying God's plan and God is in control.

Here are several questions to ponder: Do you want God to limit His solutions for your life to the scope of your understanding? Do you want Him to resolve your problems using only your ability to control your circumstances? Do you want God to limit His work in your life only to those situations, rescues, resolves, and final results to your wisdom and to events you can follow intellectually? If you say "yes" to these questions, then you choose the comfort of always knowing what is going on and what God has planned for you. Of course, the problem is your life will be limited by your knowledge or imagination, and that is very sad. If you say "no," then you surrender the comfort of comprehending life, you run the risk of losing control of your circumstances, and you will have to walk through some experiences in ignorance. At the same time, nothing will limit the amazing way God can work wonders in your life or the great things He will accomplish through you.

The truth is, God does not give us the option of always knowing His will, so we walk in ignorance through many circumstances. If we find comfort, it will not be in knowing God's next move, but it will have to be through complete confidence in Him. Jesus often tells us, "I am not asking you to *understand* what I am doing, I am asking you to trust Me." Does this last sentence remind you of a well-known proverb? *Trust in the Lord with all your heart, and lean not on your own understanding (Prov. 3:5).*

Another remedy Jesus offers the disciples' troubled hearts is the abandonment of one perspective for another. *"In My Father's house are many mansions; if it were not so, I would have told you. I go to prepare a place for you" (John 14:2).* The disciples' entire horizon was filled with despair of losing Jesus. But the Lord was telling them, "No, this is not the last horizon. There is another horizon beyond this immediate situation. That is where I am going, and that is ultimately where you will be. Because I am going now, I will have a place prepared for you when you get there. Do not be blinded by the present. My disciples, look further."

Where will you find bleakness, futility, hopelessness? In the present moment. If we have a hard time trusting Jesus, then it becomes easy to fixate on the present and obsess over what surrounds us in the moment. Our hearts are inevitably troubled and will stay troubled. What we have lost is not God, but our perspective. The temporal panorama, with its oppressive darkness, dims our eternal perspective. God is no less powerful today than yesterday, but like the sun behind a thick layer of clouds, He is momentarily hidden from our eyes. But having God hidden from our eyes should be no problem if we *walk by faith, not by sight (2 Cor. 5:7).*

Paul knew almost as much about suffering as anyone else, and he shares wisdom with troubled hearts in his letter to the Romans and the Corinthians. One of the most encouraging revelations he shares with us is that *the sufferings of this present time are not worthy to be compared with the glory which shall be revealed in us (Rom. 8:18).* Notice his reference to *this present time,* which as soon as the words are spoken is already passing away.

In a parallel passage Paul said, *For our light affliction, which is but for a moment, is working for us a far more exceeding and eternal weight of glory (2 Cor. 4:17).* We could spend a lot of time studying this verse for our own good. Our affliction is lightweight, and partly because it is temporary, *for a moment.* In the Bible, anything transitory is considered light, ethereal, vaporous (see Ps. 62:9; 146:3-4; James 4:14). If you were to place the troubles of this life on one tray of a balance scale, and on the other tray place the glory we will enjoy in eternity, the eternal side would quickly drop as far as the arm of the scale would allow it.

Paul, the beaten preacher, the imprisoned exorcist, the shipwrecked ambassador of God who was once almost executed by stoning, made reference to life's troubles as "light affliction." His hardships were not light because he was made of stone or had a high tolerance for pain, but they were light *in comparison to* God's compensations and the pleasure that awaited him. When we lose this contrast, our hearts get stuck in the troubled mode. We have to correct our perspective to ease our troubled hearts. If you do not see help around you or ahead of you, look up and trust the One who watches over you.

But Wait! There's More

The comfort I find in Jesus' promise to His disciples in this passage is this, *"And if I go and prepare a place for you, I will come again and receive you to Myself; that where I am, there you may be also" (John 14:3)*. Does that verse give you chills? Jesus Christ *wants* you to be with Him. Listen to His prayer, *"Father, I desire that they also whom You gave Me may be with Me where I am, that they may behold My glory which You have given Me; for You loved Me before the foundation of the world" (John 17:24)*. Jesus also said, "I *desire* that they . . . be with Me." Earlier in John's gospel He said, *"If anyone serves Me, let him follow Me; and where I am, there My servant will be also" (John 12:26)*. The objective is to be with Jesus; this is what He desires and it is where we will find ourselves at last.

Imagine someone offers you an all-expenses-paid tour to the Holy Land. In the desert somewhere southeast of Jerusalem, you visit a monastery, and the monks invite you into their chapel. The doorway, however, is very small, as if made for a child, and peering through it, the inside is dark and foreboding. You squeeze yourself across the threshold and enter a sacred place, decorated with the most beautiful frescoes you have ever seen. You slowly rotate your body as your mind takes in the wonder of the gospel stories, told in hand-painted artistry that doesn't seem to be of this world. Was it worth the struggle to get through the doorway? Yes, of course. You would not want to be that close and miss such splendor.

We will find ourselves coming to these difficult, annoying, and foreboding doorways throughout our Christian pilgrimage. But each time, we find the promise of sacred beauty on the other side. Jesus Christ, who is the very essence of the sacredness and beauty, will meet us with open arms as we squeeze through that last narrow passage. "I will receive you to Myself," He tells us, and it is because He desires that we should be with Him.

Jesus will come again and receive us to Himself. But what about in the meantime? The prospect of going through hardship alone so we can be with Jesus one day is comforting, but is it enough to prevent our hearts from being troubled? For some of us, just having hope is enough to keep our hearts strong and determined. Nevertheless, Jesus has provided something—or I should say, Someone—else while we wait:

> If you love Me, keep My commandments.
> And I will pray the Father, and He will give
> you another Helper, that He may abide with
> you forever—the Spirit of truth, whom the
> world cannot receive, because it neither sees
> Him nor knows Him; but you know Him,
> for He dwells with you and will be in you. I
> will not leave you as orphans; I will come to
> you.
>
> (John 14:15-18)

This promise is wonderful! Notice again the comfort comes to us by way of a Person rather than a principle or proposition. Why does Jesus say, *"another*

Helper"? Because the disciples already had a Helper, Counselor, Comforter, and Companion in Jesus Christ. But since Jesus was going away and they could not follow Him, they were facing the prospect of being abandoned, left on their own without divine companionship and support. Jesus would not allow that to happen.

The Lord, who had been the Master of every situation—from calming storms, to feeding multitudes, to raising the dead—would not leave them wondering, "What do we do now? Jesus is gone, how will we proceed? How will we remember all Jesus' teaching and how will we apply it to new situations?" Jesus' answer to these questions was the following:

> But the Helper, the Holy Spirit, whom the
> Father will send in My name, He will teach
> you all things, and bring to your
> remembrance all things that I said to you.
> Peace I leave with you, My peace I give to
> you; not as the world gives do I give to you.
> Let not your heart be troubled, neither let it
> be afraid.
>
> (John 14:26-27)

Jesus' promise of encouragement comes back around to where it began. He told them these things *before it comes* so they will know they can trust Him and believe His words of encouragement (see John 14:29). The disciples will not be alone. They will not be stranded on the earth without help, instruction, guidance, or resources. Jesus' followers will not be spiritual orphans, troubled and oppressed, but they will receive God's *Spirit of adoption* who will bear witness to their spirits that they are children of God, and will enable them to call God *Father* (see Rom. 8:15-17; Gal. 4:6-7).

Take A Deep Breath . . .

On more than one occasion I have made the foolish mistake of trying to carry the burden of the church I serve. Somehow I trick myself into thinking I have to produce solutions for every problem, resolve every crisis, produce finances for every needed purchase, work miracles, and save the world. When these oppressive delusions fill my brain, it is impossible to distinguish the little challenges from the impossible emergencies. The moment I try to take the burden of the church on my shoulders, I am instantly pressed into the ground.

Like the disciple Peter who walked on water, until he looked at it, I do well when I keep my eyes on Jesus, reminding myself that *"I am not the Christ" (John 1:20)*. As I look around our church's complex, I see all the broken hearts entering our counseling offices, all the young lives studying in our day school, and all the people walking through the sanctuary doors looking for God or a more stable walk with Him, and I start to go under. I cry, "Lord, what are we going to do?"

Then Jesus asks me, "Is that really *your* problem? If you want to handle this on your own, I can back off."

I am quick to answer, "No, Lord, please don't do that. Now that I think about it, these are *Your* problems because this is *Your* church and these are *Your* people."

"Fine," He responds, "then keep your trust in Me and everything will be fine." What a relief and joy to hear the Lord say He has already anticipated what lies ahead, given us His Spirit, and God's plan will move forward without depending on me.

I have met people who think they do not need God, that they have made their fortune themselves, and they do not need to thank anyone else for their prosperity. I have to laugh to myself at how naïve we can be about what actually holds our lives together. Do you have any idea how fragile you are? A muscle spasms in your back, a nerve is pinched, a disc slips, and you are out of commission. Think of the nerves in your spinal column as slender strands of angel-hair pasta. If one of those strands is crushed, there is no way to repair it, and it only takes minimal damage to put you in a wheelchair for the rest of your life. Is your strength a given? Your health? Your next breath?

No, the human body is a flimsy foundation for hope and confidence. A sure way to live and die with a troubled heart is to rely on yourself. But when we realize all that Jesus promised us, including God's Spirit, is with us in the same capacity that Jesus was with His disciples, then we can obey His command and not let our hearts be troubled.

"Therefore comfort one another with these words" (1 Thess. 4:18). They are much more helpful and reliable than, "Smile, brother!" or "Just hang in there."

Prayer

Lord God, our Creator;
Lord Jesus, our Savior;
Holy Spirit, our Comforter and Helper,
thank You for caring about our troubled hearts.
You know what upsets and grieves us,
You know what people, situations, and illnesses
take our spirits down.
You know what we face at home, at work, at school,
and You also know perfectly well,
that sometimes it hurts to be human.
But You have not left us alone,
nor stuck in time,
nor without hope.
You have promised us a future joy
that outweighs present sorrows.
You have given us a Companion
who teaches us the ways of Jesus,
and gives us peace.
You have asked us only for our trust through hardship.
We will not, we cannot fail,
Holy God, righteous Savior, eternal Spirit.
Amen.

CHAPTER 10

The Overwhelming Burden of Betrayal

Cast your burden on the Lord,
And He shall sustain you;
He shall never permit the righteous to be moved.

(Ps. 55:22)

Few people have gone through life without feeling the sharp pain of Julius Caesar's famous line, "Et tu, Brute?" The words are Shakespeare's; the event was Caesar's assassination in which his trusted friend, Brutus was a willing participant. The experience of betrayal is universal. As he was bleeding out from several puncture wounds, Caesar recognized his friend's face, and said, "And you, Brutus? Then fall Caesar," as if to say, "If even you have turned against me, then there really is no hope and no reason to fight for my life."

We hear a similar tone in Jesus' voice when He asks Judas, *"Friend, why have you come? Are you betraying the Son of Man with a kiss?" (Matt. 26:50; Luke 22:48)*. Jesus had made Himself vulnerable to this disciple, so Judas knew where to find Him (see John 18:1-3). The Lord's open heart allowed Judas to come close enough to assassinate Him, which is what Judas did through his betrayal.

Old Testament scholars are not convinced the titles to the Book of Psalms were written at the same time they were composed or that they reliably give insight or context for the psalms. Therefore we use the titles loosely when interpreting a psalm. In the case of Psalm 55, the title tells us this psalm was a poem given to the "Chief Musician" so he could set it to music, "with stringed instruments." The psalm serves as a *maskil*, which, according to some scholars, means an instructional poem. The Hebrew word is derived from *root* which has to do with *looking into a matter to gain wisdom or understanding.* If in the title of this psalm, *maskil* is used as a musical term, it may simply be telling us the composition will be tricky to play. If, however, it is a literary term, then we are informed that the poem calls for contemplation, which the *New King James Version* prefers.

The title also attributes this psalm to David but otherwise makes no attempt to connect it with any particular event in his life. A few scholars have suggested David wrote this poem during the revolt of his son, Absalom. We could, no doubt, link several verses with the story told in 2 Samuel 15–19; for example, the danger stalking David in the city, his flight to the wilderness, the betrayal of both Absalom and David's counselor Ahithophel, and so on. Other expressions in this psalm, however, make it seem as unlikely David had Absalom in mind.

For now, we will assume the event of Absalom's rebellion against his father lies behind this poem of contemplation. Absalom is an ambivalent character in David's story, both admirable and rascally. A remarkably attractive young man, he knew how to turn on the charm (see 2 Sam. 14:25). Absalom avenged the rape of his sister, which was his responsibility as the family's *goel*, who could be either a *redeemer* or an *avenger of blood* as the situation required. However Absalom's method of fulfilling his role went beyond vendetta and created a breach between himself and David, and resulted in temporary exile. When he returned to Judah, he set fire to the fields of Joab because he felt he was being ignored. When Joab confronted him, Absalom pressed for a meeting and reconciliation with David, which was granted.

No sooner was Absalom back in the good graces of the king, than he began a program of stealing *the hearts of the men of Judah. This task* was not that difficult because the northern tribes never felt absolute loyalty for Jerusalem's monarchy (see 2 Sam. 15:6). Absalom would *rise early and stand beside the way to the gate* and greet those who came to Jerusalem to have the king settle their legal issues. But Absalom would intercept them, pay them respect—spoil them, as it were—then tell them they had a just cause, but the king was too busy for them. However, if he were made a judge, he would take care of important issues like theirs. In other words, Absalom was playing the role of a politician, shaking hands and kissing babies (2 Sam. 15:2-6).

The Old Testament alerts us when a conspiracy is forming to seize the throne by telling us someone has *prepared for himself chariots and horsemen and fifty men to run before him (1 Kin. 1:5).* Absalom had done this very thing (see 2 Sam. 15:10), so the reader knows right away he does not have a genuine interest in the legal affairs of the men of Israel but in his own bid for the throne. He begged David's leave to go to Hebron on false grounds, then sent co-conspirators through Israel to announce his coup. Once everything was set in place, people began joining Absalom and the conspiracy *continually increased in number (2 Sam. 15:12).*

When word of Absalom's treachery reached David, he was terrified. Not wanting a blood bath in Jerusalem, and knowing he could not be safe if trapped within its walls, he decided to escape to the wilderness. David was very familiar with the desert between Judah and the Dead Sea because he had found places of refuge there when running from King Saul. So David began his exit from the city, and as he reached the Mount of Olives, a large number of his faithful servants, soldiers, and friends joined him.

If Psalm 55 reveals David's psychological state as he escaped to the desert, then we can see he entered a very dark place, because he piles up words relating to his fear: *terrors of death . . . fearfulness and trembling . . . horror has overwhelmed me.* As much as David's trust in God is a wonderful example of strength and consistency, he could still fall prey to depression, which he describes well when he says, *"My heart is severely pained within me."*

I find David's panic disappointing because he has always been my hero; manly, courageous, eager to take on giants and any other enemy who defies Israel's God. Through most of his story, it does not seem like David has any fear. More than once, he shamed Saul by sneaking up on him while the king was not looking or was asleep. David bravely led his troops into battle and distinguished himself as a military leader and worthy soldier. But now he has become an old man, a symbol of Israel's glory, and someone who does not really have the stuff to keep going to battles. Regarding his son Absalom, David's fight has gone; fear has taken its place (see Eccl. 12:1-3).

David's most renown counselor, Ahithophel, joined the revolution. How is this for salt in his wounds? Is Ahithophel's desertion what David had in mind when he penned Psalm 55:12-14?

> For it is not an enemy who reproaches me;
> Then I could bear it.
> Nor is it one who hates me who has
>   magnified himself against me;
> Then I could hide from him.
> But it was you, a man my equal,
> My companion and my acquaintance.
> We took sweet counsel together,
> And walked to the house of God in the
>   throng.

Overwhelmed, David wished for *wings like a dove* to escape the madness marching toward Jerusalem to find a place of rest (v. 6).

David's situation with Absalom certainly falls into the very, very bad day category. We also know something of his pain and despair. We have had battles with our children who seem totally blinded to our love for them, who misuse everything we have done to enable them to move toward a better life. We have been betrayed by trusted friends and stabbed in the back by people who betrayed our confidence; we have enemies who do all they can to harm us and make certain our lives are miserable. The problems continue to arrive at our doorstep until they overwhelm us. Fear takes over our hearts, and we do not know where to turn. We would love to escape, but there is nowhere to go to find peace.

A DIFFERENT LENS

Suppose for a moment this psalm has no relationship to Absalom's rebellion, and the parallels we think we see with the events of 2 Samuel 15 are merely coincidences of a number of common misfortunes. In fact, in Psalm 55:6-8, David longs to flee to the desert, but it seems to be a mere fantasy, because he wishfully speaks of what it would be like if he could do it; notice he would *fly*, *wander*, and *hasten*. We also should acknowledge he asks God to do the very thing he begged Joab not to do; namely to *Let death seize them* (v. 15, compare with 2 Sam. 18:5, 33).

Why is it so many Bible commentaries are eager to find an event from David's life to give meaning or explanation to a psalm? Inevitably, their interpretation of the psalm in light of a particular episode shades the psalm. The first reason is some Bible teachers feel most comfortable when they are dealing with very specific and concrete subjects. They do not know what to do with a passage that doesn't contain a story, a clear moral lesson, or a theological proposition. Perhaps they do not know how to read a psalm, so they feel they have to qualify it somehow and impose an external relevance to make its teaching more black and white.

Secondly, many hard-nose rationalists simply have no appreciation for poetry. This especially applies to the poetry of the Old Testament that looks quite strange to people who are familiar with the sort of rhyming, metrical verse found in greeting cards. Yet the psalms were written as poems, and God must have had some reason why He would inspire David and others to compose this type of literature. We need to learn how to appreciate each separate psalm for its own message, purpose, structure, beauty, and effect.

When you are reading a book or article, what do you do if you come to six or eight lines of poetry? Skip them? Skim over them? Read them carefully? What does poetry do to your reading of a text? Typically it slows you down. Poetry makes unconventional use of language and generally is packed with meaning. To get to the meaning you have to work harder for it. You have to slow down to be sure you are following the poet, seeing what you are supposed to see.

Our experience of life in the world, the revelation of God, the pain of tragedy, the fear of the enemy, and the challenge of faith is complex and often confusing. Simple do's and don'ts fail to help us with more complicated issues. To remind ourselves we are supposed to trust God at all times is not enough to evoke confidence in Him when our whole world is collapsing and we are running in panic. Those kinds of complications require a more sensitive and reflective type of writing than what you will find in the laws of Moses.

To get the most meaning and benefit from the psalms, we do not need to locate specific events in David's life that could have inspired his poetry, because the whole point of a psalm is the way it is supposed to touch and shed light on our lives. In fact, that is the beauty and wonder of the psalms; they speak directly to our own experience. This is also the reason poets rarely mention any specific details regarding their struggles. Who exactly is the enemy that has assaulted them? Rather than name them as the Philistines or the Moabites—and sometimes the Babylonians are named—the psalmists speak in generalities. As a result, we can apply the words of the psalm to the enemies that hound us. The same is true when the poet confesses his sins. He rarely specifies what sin he has committed, because it is enough that God knows, and readers can be free to fill in the blank with their own sin.

If we take this point of view when looking at Psalm 55, what we see is a person who is overwhelmed by distressing circumstances. He begins by asking God to *Give ear to my prayer,* and much of the rest of the psalm has to do with speech and hearing. For example, the poet *moans noisily,* but this is in response to the *voice of the enemy* (vv. 2-3). The *tongues*—which are an important speech articulator—of the wicked need to be destroyed for the violence they engender (v. 9) and the *reproaches* they have heaped on David (vv. 9, 12). The poet had at one time enjoyed *sweet counsel* with the companion who had turned against him. But the poet himself must call and *cry aloud* for God to help him, with the confidence God will hear his voice (vv. 14-19). With words smoother than butter and softer than oil, the enemy had disguised his declaration of war and hidden his drawn sword (vv. 20-21). Sometimes the enemy's only weapon is noise and our only defense is prayer (see 1 Pet. 5:6-9).

David uses many beautiful expressions to support his theme as he walks us through despair to trust. In fact the psalm ends with the commitment, *I will trust in You (v. 23)*. Whatever horrors and heartaches descend on our lives, we will always come back to trust. In fact, God sometimes empties our lives of everything else so completely that all we have left is trust. But trust in God is built upon a foundational intimacy that exists between the poet and the Lord. The psalms always assume intimacy even when the psalmist is complaining and griping, has sinned against God, or feels God abandoned him. In fact, the idea of God hiding His face is based on a prior sense of close proximity and communion (v. 1). In this particular psalm, we *feel* intimacy in the transition from verse 1 to 2, when David shifts from *Give ear to my prayer* to *Attend to me, and hear me*, as if to say, "It's *me*, Lord. It's me, Your servant who loves You."

A PLUSH RESORT

What do you think about people making God their last resort, about them trying everything else first, then if they cannot find any other way to resolve their problems, they pray? I would love for all God's children to learn that when they see danger coming or a dark cloud hanging over their homes, they can turn to God first, before looking anywhere else for help. *Cast your burden on the Lord, and He shall sustain you.* God is not a last resort, He is a plush resort.

Why do we put off calling on God when we see the tempest coming, violence rising, or friends and enemies working together to bring us down? Perhaps it is because we do not initially see that our circumstances will worsen. We think, "Oh, this is just a breeze, there's nothing to worry about." Then the wind becomes more forceful and we say, "I had better close the storm shutters." And we keep responding to the hurricane or tornado, one step at a time, assuming we can handle this situation on our own. We keep going in this mode until we reach the breaking point, and when our head starts to go under water we cry out, "Lord, save me!"

We are like the alcoholic who has not yet discovered he is an alcoholic. Others can see his drinking is interfering with his work, family relations, and spiritual progress, but he is still telling them he does not have a problem and can deal with it himself. Sometimes he is the only person who does not realize how his drinking has affected his thinking, judgment, and decision-making ability. But if you talk with him about these things, he assures you, "I can quit any time I want."

Suppose you know someone like this, and one night he calls you from a roadside where he has crashed his car. He begs you for a ride home, so you run out and get him. The next morning he feels indebted to you, so you exploit this opportunity to introduce him to an Alcoholics Anonymous fellowship. After the meeting you introduce him to a couple of people, hoping one of them will become his sponsor. But the first question they ask him is, "Do you admit that you are powerless over alcohol and your life has become unmanageable?" If he gives them the same weary line, "No, I don't have a problem. I just had a little too much last night, but I can quit anytime I want," they will smile politely and tell you, "He is not yet ready." Why? Because they know something within his nature prevents him from seeking help until he hits bottom. Once we are ready to admit our problem and our powerlessness, then helpful people will show up with all kinds of love, patience, resources, and helpful wisdom. But how sad it is that we are so stubborn we have to get to the breaking point before we confess our need for help.

What is it we are doing until we finally break and go to God for the answers and help? We are looking for some kind of escape. We are saying, *"Oh that I had wings like a dove! For then I would fly away and be at rest" (Ps. 55:6).* We want to run away; go somewhere else; become someone else; leave behind all the tension, confusion, frustration, responsibility, and friction that has made life unbearable. "If only I could go to a place where no one knows me, and those who do know me cannot find me." We escape our worsening reality until it no longer allows us to ignore its dark presence. We have waited so long, that the only prayer left is of total desperation. We break down before God and cry out, *My heart is severely pained within me.* Then what?

Take a slow, deep breath before you read this next
verse. *He has redeemed my soul in peace from the battle
that was against me (v. 18).*

The plush resort should have been our first rather
than last choice. How much insanity could we have
avoided if we only prayed sooner? And yet, how
wonderful it is to know that as long as we have
breath, it is not too late to call on God.

ARE YOU STILL CARRYING THAT?

In the middle of the chaos and deep sadness of this
psalm comes a word of advice from the poet—*Cast
your burden on the Lord, and He shall sustain you; He shall
never permit the righteous to be moved (Ps. 55:22).* These
burdens awaken us in the middle of the night, churn-
ing our minds, tormenting our hearts, refusing to permit us to go back to sleep. Throw those burdens on
God and not one of them will be too much for Him;
they will not confound or overwhelm Him. Your burdens are not a burden for God. Throw your burden on
Him in prayer, like the poet did, and if you have to,
keep throwing it on Him *evening and morning and at
noon (v. 17).* He cannot hear your cry for help if you do
not cry out to Him. But cry, and God will hear; He will
sustain you and not leave you under that burden (vv.
3, 19).

We have trusted our own strength, and found it to
be insufficient. What is my strength? It's nothing to
the wave breaking over me, the rock falling on me, the
bolt of lightning crashing next to me. What is God's
strength? We cannot know; there is no measurement

in our possession that can gauge His strength. We can only say what His strength is *not*—it is not limited, localized, stoppable, beatable, and so on. Return to the city streets or the battlefield, return to confront the enemy or the treacherous friend, return to the voice of reproach and the hand of oppression, not trusting in your own strength, but trusting in the Lord's strength, which is omnipotent. Are we able to face this brutal season of life? No, but God is able. *Cast your burden on Him and He will sustain you.*

God's peace floods our lives when we no longer seek to dictate the outcome of our trials. We leave the problem with Him and say, "Whatever You think best, Lord. Whatever pleases You most. Whatever will win Your honor and bring me closer to You in peace and joy." When we surrender—really surrender, even our insistence that God makes our lives turn out a certain way—then we fall into peace. The secret is not to *attain* peace, but to *be* in the peace of God that already surrounds us. Is your anxiety keeping you from peace? Then give it up and peace will pour over you. Is your burden keeping you from peace? Throw it on the Lord, and it will no longer stop up the mouth of the well.

Prayer

Our Heavenly Father,
from the darkness of our confusion,
the pressure of our burdens,
the disappointment of disloyal friends,
the threats of the enemy,

and the severe pain of our hearts,
we escape, not to the wilderness, but to You.
No other refuge than Your love,
no other resort than Your grace,
no other confidence than Your strength;
we will trust in You.
Sustain us.
Keep us stable.
And for those in despair,
awaken them to Your presence
that deliverance is at the door
if they will turn the handle with their prayers.
Lift us up into Your peace as we cast our burdens
on You.
Through Jesus' trustworthy name.
Amen.

CHAPTER 11

Putting Suffering to Good Use

Blessed be the God and Father of our Lord
Jesus Christ, the Father of mercies and God
of all comfort, who comforts us in all our
tribulation, that we may be able to comfort
those who are in any trouble, with the
comfort with which we ourselves are
comforted. For as the sufferings of Christ
abound in us, so our consolation also
abounds through Christ. Now if we are
afflicted, it is for your consolation and
salvation, which is effective for enduring the
same sufferings which we also suffer. Or if
we are comforted, it is for your consolation
and salvation. And our hope for you is
steadfast, because we know that as you are
partakers of the sufferings, so also you will
partake of the consolation.

(2 Cor. 1:3-7)

Have you heard the following question? "If God is all-
wise, all-good, and all-powerful, then why is there so

much evil and suffering in the world?" Of all the reasons people give for not believing in God, this is the one most frequently given and most difficult to answer. Even Christians who are familiar with the introduction of pain and evil into the world through the Garden of Eden have difficulty understanding and explaining why a God so loving and merciful would permit suffering at all, much less the excess of suffering this planet witnesses every day.

We are not immune from suffering—not for the poor or rich, the infant or the elderly, the innocent or the guilty. Even God's children who have come to Him through Jesus Christ, who believe in Him, trust in Him, and obey Him have no special protection from pain and sorrow or violence caused by human or natural forces. Paul, who was a radically devoted servant of God, speaks in the introduction to his second letter to the Corinthians about his own suffering. Suffering is universal.

EXPLANATIONS THAT LEAD TO DEAD ENDS

Unfortunately some Christians have not applied careful biblical research or critical thinking to the problem of pain, yet they are enthusiastically prepared to tell you why you are sick or permanently injured. Even though a person may think they are suffering unjustly, these Christian crusaders, like Job's friends, are prepared to tell the sick or disabled believer their affliction has a sinful cause. They are convinced children of God were meant to live pain-free lives, and if they are not then they have committed a sin, omitted a spiritual duty, or they lack the faith they should have in God. If only it were that simple.

The disciples held a similar viewpoint, and when they passed a man who had been blind from birth, they raised an intriguing theological difficulty. *"Rabbi, who sinned, this man or his parents, that he was born blind?" (John 9:2).* The man's blindness posed a theological riddle, so they went straight to theories of prenatal and congenital disabilities to work out the tough questions. But they failed to raise or totally ignored a tougher question, "What can we do for this poor man who has been blind his entire life?" Of course, they could not heal him, the idea never passed their minds. They could help him get around, but they were engaged in the demanding business of following Jesus. So since they either could not or would not do anything to assist this young man, they theologized his blindness.

Jesus dismissed their theological speculations with one word, *"Neither."* The man's blindness had nothing to do with sin, neither his own nor anyone else's. *"Neither this man nor his parents sinned, but that the works of God should be revealed in him" (John 9:3).* The man's sin did not cause his blindness and his faith did not heal him. In fact, he had no idea Jesus would heal him or that He *could* heal him. Righteous people suffer. Unrighteous people sometimes escape suffering. These were issues that vexed Job, a *blameless and upright* man who *feared God and shunned evil* from start to finish (see Job 1:1; 21:7-21).

Consider Hebrews 11, which some commentators refer to as a Believer's Hall of Fame or Hall of Faith.

Each name entered into the record represented people who had distinguished themselves for their outstanding faith in God. Yet some were mocked, scourged, imprisoned, stoned, sawn in two, wandered about in deserts dressed in goatskin clothing; they were *destitute, afflicted, tormented,* and *wandered in deserts and mountains, in dens and caves of the earth (Heb. 11:37-38).* The testimony of their faith and lives in God undermines any argument that tries to assert people of faith do not suffer but have a special bubble of protection around them at all times.

Nevertheless, I admit it is tempting to assume sin is somehow at the root of disaster when I hear of someone's misfortune. But even more so, when suffering visits me, the first words out of my mouth are, "What have I done wrong?" Even though I know Job suffered immense loss and pain for no reason, I still think there must be a reason why I am sick or in pain, and I want to know why God is angry me, has left me, or has sent hardship into my life—as if He had nothing better to do than torment me.

When one of my granddaughters was around four years old, she began asking, "What did I deserve to do this?" Her mangled version of the familiar question became a frequent slogan around our home. If God loves me, and bad things happen to me, then I must deserve the trouble that has come my way. If I do not deserve it and God loves me, then the problem is even greater and more difficult to solve because it would seem pain and evil are mostly senseless, irrational, and without good purpose. I would rather think bad experiences are the result of my own actions because that would at least make sense and give me the illusion of control. If I brought this tragedy on myself, then I can make it go away.

But if God loves me, controls all the circumstances of my life, and I can please Him by walking in His truth, then why were my dad and brother killed in a plane crash? And my mother, who, next to my wife, is the most godly woman I have ever known, why did she suffer and die with cancer? Why are Christian women raped? Why are Christian missionaries kidnapped and killed by rebel forces? I have a difficult time dealing with these inequities and wonder why would God allow them to happen.

THE "WHY?" QUESTION

Remember Jesus' prayer in the Garden of Gethsemane? *"Abba, Father, all things are possible for You. Take this cup away from Me" (Mark 14:36).* Does it sound like Jesus knows confusing sorrow that says, "God, You can prevent this misery. You can relieve Me right now from my torment. You can do all things, so if You love me, find another way to accomplish Your will than through my agony"? Obviously God does not take the cup of suffering from His children, but if He loves us—as indeed He loved His Son—why does He make us drink the "cup"?

Listen to the way Martha scolded Jesus after her brother Lazarus died. She sounds exactly like we do, and she uses the same words we have used, *"Lord, if You had been here, my brother would not have died" (John 11:21).* Does that sound familiar? "Lord, if only You

had come when I called You . . ." "If only You had answered our prayers sooner." "If only You had caused
the car to swerve rather than plow down that child,"
and so on. I am forced to confess in the grind of the
daily lives of people in my church, I really do not
know and cannot answer their "Why?" questions.

However, in the case of Lazarus, Jesus' answer became abundantly clear and highlights forever the
most encouraging words ever spoken in human history, *"I am the resurrection and the life. He who believes in
Me, though he may die, he shall live. And whoever lives and
believes in Me shall never die"* (John 11:25-26).

Here is some really important news. Although we
cannot help asking the "Why?" questions, in almost
every instance of suffering, answers are not immediate, rational, nor visible. To ask the question is one of
the most useless things we can do in the face of suffering. It distracts us from the more important questions, like, "What do I do in response to this current
crisis?"; "What am I learning through all of this?";
"Where is God?"; and "What is He doing?" To get
stuck in the unanswerable "Why?" questions interferes with the grief process, stalls our growth, and eats
away at our trust in God.

WHY PAIN IS A PROBLEM

If I did not believe in God, pain and evil would not be
a riddle to me. I would simply shrug it off and say,
"That's the way the ball bounces," "I guess it was
meant to be," or "You win some, lose some." I would
resign myself to fate and an impersonal and mindless

universe in which no one wonders why good or evil exists because everything is a matter of interpretation. But since I do not believe in blind chance and I do believe God loves me supremely, suffering is a problem. I would certainly not stand by and let my children suffer the way God lets me suffer if it were in my power to *take the cup* from them.

Paul closes a challenging section of his letter to the Romans with these words of praise:

> Oh, the depth of the riches both of the
> wisdom and knowledge of God! How
> unsearchable are His judgments and His
> ways past finding out!
> For who has known the mind of the
> Lord?
> Or who has become His counselor?
> Or who has first given to Him
> And it shall be repaid to him?
>
> For of Him and through Him and to Him
> are all things, to whom be glory forever.
> Amen.
>
> (Rom. 11:33-36)

I have spent many frustrating hours trying to sort out God's ways. But Paul was right, God's ways are past finding out, as He affirmed through His prophet Isaiah:

> "For My thoughts are not your thoughts,
> Nor are your ways My ways," says the
> Lord.

"For as the heavens are higher than the
      earth,
So are My ways higher than your ways,
And My thoughts than your thoughts."

(Is. 55:8-9)

IF I WERE GOD

If the position of God were put to a vote, pious Christians would likely vote for me, because if I were God, I would bless everyone who believed in me. The moment a person put his trust in me, I would dump so many good things into his life, he would be laughing nonstop for a million years. Believers would never get sick, injured, sad, or even come near death. I would shield them from every hurt and disappointment. No one on earth would be able to resist believing in me, because I would impoverish, starve, and torture unbelievers while sending prosperity, abundance, and pleasure on believers. I would not make my *sun rise on the evil and on the good and sends rain on the just and the unjust (Matt. 5:45)*. Only my friends would receive my blessings and everyone else would suffer. And, of course, everyone would want to be my friend. Or would they? Could I know whether anyone really loved me?

I have provided biblical counsel to a multi-millionaire who lives in Newport Beach, California. The last time he visited with me, he told me his most recent marriage had fallen apart and even though a new coterie of women were throwing themselves at him, he was dejected. "I can't know if a woman really loves *me* or is in love with everything I can afford to give her."

How miserable would life be if we could never discern a person's true feelings for us? "Do you love *me*," we would wonder, "or do you love a purpose I fulfill for you? Do you want *me* or am I a means to an end?" If the wealthy man had nothing to offer a woman other than his soul and body, and she wanted to be with him more than any other man in the world, then he would have no difficulty in discerning the authenticity of her love. My belief is he would do well to give away everything he owns to his former wives, his children, and to charity, then seek true love. Solomon said it well, *If a man would give for love all the wealth of his house, it would be utterly despised (Song 8:7).*

Apart from the hardship of real trials, how would God know we loved Him? In Jeremiah, God reminisces on an earlier period in Israel's history:

> I remember you,
> The kindness of your youth,
> The love of your betrothal,
> When you went after Me in the wilderness,
> In a land that was not sown.
> Israel was holiness to the Lord,
> The firstfruits of His increase.
>
> (Jer. 2:2-3)

When God says *Israel was holiness to the Lord*, He does not mean they were sinless or especially sacred, but their devotion to Him made them and their worship acceptable. Anything devoted to God became holy. They became holy because they *went after* Him! Where did they go? Into a palace? Into a garden paradise like Eden? No, but into the wilderness, *a land that was not sown*; that is, without vegetation to feed them.

Many young couples begin marriage in this same way. For bookshelves they have cinder blocks and two by six boards. For furniture, they have whatever discards they can find. They live in the cheapest apartment they can find. And they are utterly happy, because they have each other without conditions, without calculating personal benefits, without needing anything but love to sustain them. God told Israel, "I remember those days, and they were our best years together."

God allows me to suffer and to experience setbacks, disappointments, and grief. When these enter my life, I am faced with a choice: I can give up on God because I am not clear how He could be good, loving, and powerful, yet let crushing sorrow fill my heart. Or I can continue to trust Him, believing my circumstances do not tell me the truth about His feeling toward me. To know He loves me, I must rely on what He has revealed in Scripture.

Charles Spurgeon once said that everything we experience is exactly what we would choose for ourselves if only we were as wise and loving as God. Of course we do not have God's unlimited knowledge or perspective and can see only what is immediately before our eyes. But . . .

If we could see beyond today as God can
    see,
If all the clouds should roll away, the
    shadows flee.
O'er present griefs we would not fret,
Each sorrow we would soon forget,
For many joys are waiting yet, for you and
    me.

If we could know beyond today as God
    doth know,
Why dearest treasures pass away and tears
    must flow.
And why the darkness leads to light,
Why dreary days will soon grow bright,
Some day life's wrongs will be made right,
    faith tells us so.

If we could see, if we could know, we often
    say,
But God in love a veil doth throw across our
    way.
We cannot see what lies before, and so we
    cling to Him the more,
He leads us till this life is o'er, trust and
    obey.

> "Beyond Today"
> Norman J. Clayton

    So if I were God, I would completely ruin every-
thing because there could be no choice; no love; no

trust; and no hope of progress, growth, or development. We would be stuck in a mechanistic universe without categories for grace, mercy, or even enthusiasm and spontaneous joy. We need a universe exactly like the one we now inhabit, even with its injustice and apparent random instances of suffering, to discover true goodness, beauty, and love. We need the universe to be as it is to promote spiritual growth and change; otherwise, our natural laziness will prevent spiritual growth.

We learned earlier no matter how well Alcoholics Anonymous assists people to sobriety, *nothing* works for the alcoholic until he has hit bottom. Human nature does not strive for improvement unless forced into it. We tend to settle into life as it is, even when it's less than pleasant, simply because we believe we can cope with our current issues. We cannot imagine what we would do with a different set of circumstances. For that reason, some people prefer to live with disabilities rather than accept possible cures. The threat of the unknown creates greater fear than living in familiar misery (consider the otherwise puzzling question of Jesus to the disabled man in John 5:6, *"Do you want to be made well?"*).

Human nature resists change unless forced into it by pain. Although I disagree often with Abraham Maslow's philosophy of psychology, one statement he made has my full agreement, "I (and others) have been increasingly impressed with the fact that tragedy can sometimes be therapeutic, and that therapy often seems to work best when people are *driven* into it by pain. It is when the shallow life doesn't work that it is

questioned and that there occurs a call to fundamen-
tals."* Unless the pain of staying in the same condition
is greater than the pain of changing, we will not
change. The wonder of human stubbornness in Scripture is God sometimes makes a person's life unbearable in hopes of driving them to repentance, but *the
people do not turn to Him who strikes them (Is. 9:13).*

I do not think we have given sufficient thought that
God does not take any pleasure in human suffering
and death; His preference is that no one *should perish
but that all should come to repentance (2 Pet. 3:9).* Listen
to the plaintive tone in God's voice when He says
through the prophet Ezekiel, *"As I live," says the Lord
God, "I have no pleasure in the death of the wicked, but that
the wicked turn from his way and live. Turn, turn from
your evil ways! For why should you die, O house of Israel?"
(Ezra 33:11).* What happens when God remains silent,
when He puts off punishment, when He withholds
the consequence of sin? He explains, *These things you
have done, and I kept silent; You thought that I was alto-
gether like you (Ps. 50:21* and see also vv. 16-23).

PAUL'S PAINFUL AUTOBIOGRAPHY

Paul was neither an amateur nor theorist when it
came to suffering. When Jesus told Ananias to go meet
Paul, pray for and baptize him, Jesus said, *"For I will
show him how many things he must suffer for My name's
sake" (Acts 9:16).* Imagine on the very day you came to

---

* Abraham Maslow, *Toward a Psychology of Being* (New York, NY: Van
Nostrand Reinhold Company, 1968), 14.

faith in Christ, you knew you would face *chains and tribulations* for the rest of your life? *(Acts 20:22-23)*.

In 2 Corinthians 1 Paul mentions *tribulation, suffering, affliction* . . . he knew them all. In chapters 11 and 12, he produces a long list of harrowing and painful experiences that would convince most of us we had chosen the wrong vocation. Paul did not go through these terrible hardships merely to prove he was an apostle. He saw a different purpose for them, which served the benefit of those who followed his ministry. Because he received God's comfort in his tribulation, he was able to comfort others who were in any sort of trouble. In other words, Paul saw more than a hope for the future that helped him survive painful situations, he saw a positive value in the pain and divine comfort that followed.

God softened Paul's heart through suffering, taught him empathy for others who endured the same sufferings, and enabled him to give something of real value to those who need comfort, consolation, reassurance, and salvation. The same is true for all God's ministers. How can we comfort someone in their grief if we have never grieved? To say, "I understand" to someone who is depressed, when we do not know the first thing about how it feels to be depressed, is cheap assurance, and they can see right through it. But when the One who is known as *A Man of sorrows and acquainted with grief* tells you, "I understand," you can see by the pain in His eyes that He really does, and that brings infinite comfort (see Is. 53:3).

The people who belong to the fraternity of grief and

suffering can recognize each other, and the level of their empathy is unreachable. No one wants to undergo the initiation, nor would anyone choose to belong to this fraternity, but life often offers us no choice. Once you have been initiated, you become qualified to walk alongside others through their fiery ordeals. The initiation is exactly what makes Jesus Christ our perfect High Priest:

> Therefore, in all things He had to be made like His brethren, that He might be a merciful and faithful High Priest in things pertaining to God, to make propitiation for the sins of the people. For in that He Himself has suffered, being tempted, He is able to aid those who are tempted. We do not have a High Priest who cannot sympathize with our weaknesses, but was in all points tempted as we are, yet without sin.
>
> (Heb. 2:17-18; 4:15)

Unless I had been down this road myself, how could I empathize with someone who is so broke they cannot afford another meal, they are unable to pay their rent, and their car is likely to be repossessed? And how could I comfort them if I had not discovered the blessed work of God's Spirit encouraging, strengthening, and comforting me? Having experienced God's help, I am able to reassure others God has not forgotten them but will provide His help and grace.

The suffering God walks us through—and He is *with us* all the way through the *valley of the shadow of death*—not only proves the sincerity of my love for God, but enables me to understand and empathize with the pain and grief of others. Even though sharing heartache with another person has a sad part, there is incredible joy in telling them about God's care through the darkness, His merciful rescue, and the grace that makes me a stronger, better person than I was before. The psalmist said, *Before I was afflicted I went astray, but now I keep Your word (Ps. 119:67)*. Because I have been there, I can guarantee others God loves them, He has not abandoned them, He is in control, and He will bring them through their ordeal.

Everyone has problems, goes through stressful and unpleasant seasons in life, experiences heartbreaking losses, and eventually stands face-to-face with death. Everyone has problems, but not everyone responds to their problems with the same resources and confidence. Some people have nowhere to turn when they lose a loved one to death; no place of comfort or hope. Some of God's children find Him to be their *strength, rock, fortress, deliverer,* and *salvation* in whom they trust *(Ps. 18:1-2)*. These worshipers of the living God are immune to pain and sorrow, but they have an unknown resource to those who have not entrusted God with their lives. When a child of God suffers, *the Father of mercies and the God of all comfort* meets them in their broken state, binds their wounds, reveals His tenderness, and leads them to a new horizon (see Ps. 107:4-22; 136:23). For all the challenges of hanging on to faith in God in light of pain and evil, I would not live

apart from Him. I am so grateful I can retreat to His
throne of grace to *obtain mercy and find grace to help in
time of need (Heb. 4:16).*

Prayer

Teach us, O Lord,
how trusting in You results in real help,
while bringing pleasure to Your heart.
Thank You for the open door,
the throne of grace,
the bridge of prayer.
We bring to You the mess we have made of our lives;
do what You can with them—
put the broken pieces together,
weave the loose ends into a beautiful tapestry—
for You can do far more with a damaged life
than anyone else could do with a perfect human.
Lead us through our pain and sorrow
into a whole new dimension of life with You.
We are eager to get through this dark season,
and to the better place You have chosen for us,
in Christ Jesus our Lord.
Amen.

CHAPTER 12

The Presence in the Storm

Now when neither sun nor stars appeared
for many days, and no small tempest beat
on us, all hope that we would be saved was
finally given up. But after long abstinence
from food, then Paul stood in the midst of
them and said, "Men, you should have
listened to me, and not have sailed from
Crete and incurred this disaster and loss.
And now I urge you to take heart, for there
will be no loss of life among you, but only
the ship. For there stood by me this night an
angel of the God I serve, saying, 'Do not be
afraid, Paul; you must be brought before
Caesar; and indeed God has granted you all
those who sail with you.' Therefore take
heart, men, for I believe God that it will be
just as it was told me."

(Acts 27:20-25)

Every time we lead a tour to Turkey and Greece to follow Paul's footsteps, at least one person in our group
complains. The food is not to their liking, their room
is too noisy, the sites were not at all what they ex-

pected, the souvenirs are too expensive, and so on. But if those same whiners had sailed with Paul on the trip Luke describes in Acts 27, they would have been kissing our tour guide's feet the whole way there and back. If you ever board a ship bound for Greece and Turkey, make certain to avoid the cruise line Paul chose.

Paul was a prisoner of Rome on his way to the capital city to present his case to Caesar. He was put in the custody of Julius, *a centurion of the Augustan Regiment (Acts 27:1).* The selection of Julius turned out to be fortunate because the centurion apparently respected the apostle, treated him kindly, and allowed him certain liberties (v. 3).

They boarded an Alexandrian cargo ship in the port of Myra, hauling wheat to Italy. Sailing was difficult once they left the coast and headed into open water. They fought a headwind the whole way, which required them to do a lot of tacking back and forth. Finally they arrived at *a place called Fair Havens (v. 7).* The fall weather made further travel dangerous, and Paul, a veteran traveler, told the centurion as much, but he was *more persuaded by the helmsman and the owner of the ship than by the things spoke by Paul (vv. 9-11).*

A soft wind from the south seemed fortuitous to the captain and navigator, so they hoisted the sails and left the safety of the harbor. But they quickly discovered how foolish they had been to venture out on the Mediterranean during this season, and the ship was hit by *a tempestuous head wind called Euroclydon*—a northeastern storm. They fought the storm as long as they could, but finally gave up and let the wind have its way.

The weather did not abate, so tying down the rigging, they began to discard everything else. A few days later, having no idea where they were (they had not seen the sun during the day or the stars at night), and still beaten by the tempest, *all hope that we would be saved was finally given up (vv. 13-20).*

At this critical hour, Paul came forward and through howling wind made an announcement. Never underestimate the value of having a man or woman of God on board when the weather turns ugly. We may not know what the storm will do to our ship, but knowing someone is praying and listening to God can be a great encouragement.

Paul was not one of those I-told-you-so type of people—well, maybe he was—but he shouted over the wind and the rain, *"Men, you should have listened to me" (Acts 27:21).* He then told them an angel of the God he served had reassured him, that though the ship and its cargo would be lost, God would preserve Paul so he could complete his assigned mission. God had graciously given him every other passenger and crewman on board. "Take heart," he encouraged them, "for I believe God."

THE CONSTANTS

Our life situation is as different from Paul's as east is from west and ancient is from modern. Nevertheless, constant and basic circumstances hold true for every human who is beset by harrowing or stressful circumstances. Walking back through this story, we notice some of the underlying realities relevant to our voyage through the storm.

First, the storm that beat down was not Paul's fault. He was on board that ship because he was a prisoner. He was sailing in the beginning of winter because the centurion and captain would not listen to him. And he certainly had no control over the weather.

I have been in ministry and the Lord's service for many years, and I have learned a few things in this area. If you think your circumstances will move painlessly, effortlessly, and smoothly because you know what God wants you to do and you are busy with His work, you will be in for a shock. I have seen people apply themselves to a mission or ministry, convinced they are doing God's will, but quickly giving up when they cannot raise sufficient funds, run into legal red tape, or people criticize their dream or method of pursuing it. They are like the rocky soil Jesus described, who *when hear the word, immediately receive it with gladness*, but *when tribulation or persecution arises for the word's sake, immediately they stumble* (Mark 4:16-17).

So, you have put your hand to the plow, have you? You have set sail on the high seas on an adventure with God. Now you are expecting sunny skies, a stiff breeze, and smooth sailing all the way. Forgive me for disenchanting you of that lovely fantasy, but read again the episode Mark reports when the disciples took Jesus *along in the boat as He was. And other little boats were also with Him. And a great windstorm arose, and the waves beat into the boat, so that it was already fill-*

ing (Mark 4:36-37). You can be on a mission for God, you can be sailing the direction He wants you to go, you can even have Jesus on board with you, but you can still be hit so soundly by a storm that your ship takes on water and begins to sink.

Remember the words Jesus said, *"If the world hates you, you know that it hated Me before it hated you . . . . Remember the word that I said to you, 'A servant is not greater than his master.' If they persecuted Me, they will also persecute you. If they kept My word, they will keep yours also" (John 15:18, 20).*

"Speak to Us Smooth Things"

"Come on, Chuck! Don't we get some kind of special pass? Doesn't God charm our lives with grace so we can live in a bubble of protection unlike the rest of humanity? Isn't there some kind of immunity card we're supposed to receive as Christians so nothing can touch us, whether natural disaster, bacterial invasion, or human cruelty?" I would certainly be first in line to sign up for that kind of Christian life, but it simply does not exist, and God never promises anything like that. Here is the truth: You will have terrifying and deadly storms. Jesus' promise is not, "There will be no storms for those who do My will," but rather, "I will be with you through the storms." I find great comfort Paul could say, *"For there stood by me this night an angel of the God to whom I belong and whom I serve" (Acts 27:23).* The Lord was on board the ship in which Paul sailed, *with* him in the storm.

Return to the disciples on the Sea of Galilee when

the storm arose. They realized no matter how much water they bailed, they were not getting anywhere. In a panic, they woke Jesus and asked Him, *"Teacher, do You not care that we are perishing?" (Mark 4:38)*. After shutting down the wind and waves, Jesus said to them, *"Why are you so fearful? How is it that you have no faith?"* You would think witnessing a drama like this would put their hearts at ease, but Mark says, *And they feared exceedingly, and said to one another, "Who can this be, that even the wind and the sea obey Him!" (Mark 4:41)*. Make no mistake, even when we are in the center of God's will, the storms are terrifying. The angel would not have said, *"Do not be afraid, Paul" (Acts 27:24)* unless Paul was afraid.

If one of life's storms hits you so hard you become afraid you will not survive it, that *all hope that you will be saved is finally given up (v. 20)*, and you despair *even of life* and feel the *sentence of death* within yourself *(2 Cor. 1:9)*, then understand God has His will in the storm and He is teaching you *that we should not trust in ourselves but in God who raises the dead, who delivered us from so great a death, and does deliver us; in whom we trust that He will still deliver us (2 Cor. 1:9-10)*. Do not forget it always helps to get a lot of people praying for you when you are driven to despair (see 2 Cor. 1:11).

Paul announced to the sailors and soldiers the angel told him he *must* be brought before Caesar and they *must* run aground on a certain island (see Acts 27:24, 26). These two *musts* established the certainty of their survival and were as real and reliable as the wind, rain, and waves that hammered their ship. The storms *must* come, but God's will *must* also be done.

I have been caught in storms from which I thought I would never emerge. I've had moments when I figured, "This is the end. I guess my work for God is finished because I'm not going to survive this storm. This is what death feels like." Perhaps God smiled as He said, "Oh, no, Smith, it will not be that easy. Giving up in the storm would certainly require less faith and hard work, but I'm not done with you yet. I'll let you know when it's time to come home, but for now, don't be afraid and don't give up so easily; it is a discredit to you and dishonor to Me."

WHAT DOESN'T KILL ME . . . WHAT WILL IT DO?

Is there an evangelical Christian in North America who has not heard one of J. Vernon McGee's sermons? Read this sentence, then quickly look away from the page and give yourself 10 seconds to recall the hymn that opens his radio program. Now! . . . .

I only bring up the hymn, "How Firm a Foundation," to quote one of its verses:

> When through fiery trials thy pathway shall
>   lie,
> My grace all-sufficient shall be thy supply;
> The flame shall not hurt thee; I only design
> Thy dross to consume, and thy gold to
>   refine.

The storm is not meant to destroy you, the flood is not meant to drown you, and the fire is not meant to consume you. Its purpose is to purify your soul; remove the negative and destructive thoughts from your mind; and strengthen your heart with God's mercy, grace, love, and peace.

God's purpose for Paul did not lie *in* the storm, but *through* the storm. His plan and purpose never take a holiday, never stop moving, and never walk away from a project before it is finished. But while we are in the storm, we do not have any idea what divine purpose it might serve. Did Paul know why he had to go through a storm before reaching Rome? We can't be sure God's purpose was clear *during* the storm, but if we turn a page and read the next chapter, it becomes clear. God was interested in Paul's appearance before Caesar, but He also wanted a community of islanders to see the power of Jesus in action, to receive healing, and, in turn, to provide Paul and his traveling companions necessary supplies for their journey (see Acts 28:1-10).

Perhaps you have heard someone say, "I was told to cheer up, things could always be worse. So I cheered up, and sure enough, things got worse!" That's almost exactly what happened to Paul. After his pep talk, more drifting in the sea, and nearing an unseen land mass, the sailors had a meal at Paul's urging and *they were all encouraged* (vv. 33-36). But here is a disturbing turn of events. Afterward, when it looked like everyone could make it to shore, the Roman soldiers planned on killing all the prisoners—including Paul— so that none of them would swim away and escape (vv. 42-43). Then, when Paul finally reached shore safely, a deadly viper bit him. By now Paul had already been through so much drama, he could not even make himself care about one more unbelievable mishap. As if to say, "What else?!" he merely *shook off the creature into the fire and suffered no harm (Acts 28:5).*

Is your life shadowed by dark clouds? Have you finally given up all hope? Did you survive the storm to be threatened by an over-eager soldier or bitten by a snake? Do not agitate yourself or fry brain cells by trying to sort it all out. But tell yourself, "It feels like my life is out of control, driven by this storm. The truth, however, is that I am not being aimlessly driven, but divinely directed. No doubt I will land on some island where someone will need to see Jesus' power and love. Then the God who kept me through the storm, the sword, and the snake, will so work in my life to meet the needs of the islanders.

Too bad we cannot turn the page of our lives and sneak a peek at the next chapter. But who knows? Perhaps what God has planned next would seem even more horrific or impossible, and we are better off not knowing anything else. He will complete the good work He has begun in us, He is able to keep what we have committed to Him, and His peace that surpasses all understanding will guard our hearts and minds through Christ Jesus (see Phil. 1:6; 4:7; 2 Tim. 1:12). We will never outgrow our need to trust God.

While he was in prison in Rome, Paul wrote to the Philippian Christians and explained to them . . .

> . . . that the things which happened to me
> have actually turned out for the furtherance
> of the gospel, so that it has become evident
> to the whole palace guard and to all the rest,

> that my chains are in Christ; and most of the
> brethren in the Lord, having become
> confident by my chains, are much more bold
> to speak the word without fear.
>
> (Phil. 1:12-14)

Hindsight is the enlightened view of our circumstances. Unfortunately, we have to keep going through the hard stuff until we reach that vantage point. God was in prison with Paul back in Jerusalem and Caesarea, when he became discouraged that due process was taking so long and was being misused by his accusers. God was in the storm with Paul when everyone on board despaired of surviving. God was with Paul swimming to shore, building a fire, bit by a snake, healing the magistrate, and all the other islanders who came to receive God's touch. In all those crazy events, from drama on the high seas to *perils of waters, in perils of robbers, in perils of my own countrymen, in perils of the Gentiles, in perils in the city, in perils in the wilderness, in perils in the sea, in perils among false brethren*, God was promoting the furtherance of the gospel *(2 Cor. 11:26)*.

ANOTHER TROPHY FOR GOD?

In the beginning of this story, we were briefly introduced to Julius, the centurion responsible for getting Paul to Rome. We saw he granted Paul liberty to visit with friends and protected him from the deadly intentions of the soldiers (see Acts 27:3, 43). But what do you suppose Julius thought of everything he witnessed?

God handled beautifully all the troubles—many of which Julius shared—that came crashing down on Paul. Julius witnessed Paul's prophetic warning, the message he received from God's angel, the incident with the viper, the healing of Publius, and the other people who were healed, In fact, Julius was with Paul from Caesarea in Palestine until he handed him over to the captain of the guard in Rome (see Acts 28:16).

Is it possible Julius became one of those believers within the Roman legion who put his faith in Christ based on what he witnessed in Paul's life? If so, it's interesting that it would not matter whether Paul despaired of life—until the angel stood by him; sharing an experience like that with Paul would only make Julius feel an even stronger bond with him. If Julius did not become a believer based on what he saw in Paul's life, a stronger argument for surrendering one's life to Christ could not be made than the way God took Paul through the storm.

Caught in a storm? The Lord stands by you, the Lord's purpose sustains you, and His Word will encourage and guide you through the darkness. Is your ship lunging in the waves? Get a firm grip on a secure line and do not let go until the sun reappears. The Lord's promise—that He would never leave us nor forsake us—is as secure a line as you could wish to have in your hand. Put your face in the wind until the salt water runs from your chin and shout to the clouds, "I believe God!" Then encourage others who are afraid and despairing of life. Do these things, and when the seas are again calm, the clouds part, and the world is beautiful, you will rejoice that your trust held firm, you brought honor to your Heavenly Father, and someone is closer to God.

Prayer

Father, what is the storm?
The thunder is Your voice,
the lightning is Your servant,
the wind is the wild power of Your Spirit.
We have been misreading the weather!
We thought, "All these things are against me!"
In fact, all these things have been working for us,
because the storm rises and falls at Your command.
So use the storm as You see fit, O Lord.
Refine, purify, knock off the rough edges of
our character,
and make our faith solid.
Strengthen our ability to trust You,
and increase our influence in helping others to
trust You.
We would love to rush into the next chapter of
our lives,
to discover that exciting work Your Spirit
has undertaken,
and for what the storm is preparing us;
but give us grace to live with integrity in this
present chapter.
Sustain us with Your presence.
In the name of the storm-Master,
Jesus Christ our Lord.
Amen.

Benediction

May the Lord be with you and
bless you and keep you in His love.
May you know
the comfort of the Father's love,
the presence of the Son in suffering,
and the strength of the Spirit to hope, trust, and obey.
May God ease the burden of your heart,
may He reduce the troubles in your life,
and shelter you from the stormy blast.
The Lord send forth His light and truth,
lead you to His dwelling place,
and secure you in His power,
until the day when you pass through the final storm
and arrive on His heavenly shore.
In the name of the Father, and of the Son, and of the
Holy Spirit.
Amen.

Scripture Index